RAMBLINGS, RANTS,

— *and* —

RAVINGS OF A MAN

As Viewed and Lived through
the Eyes of a Guy

GEORGE ROBBINS

iUniverse LLC
Bloomington

RAMBLINGS, RANTS, AND RAVINGS OF A MAN
AS VIEWED AND LIVED THROUGH THE EYES OF A GUY

iUniverse books may be ordered through booksellers or by contacting:

iUniverse
1663 Liberty Drive
Bloomington, IN 47403
www.iuniverse.com
1-800-Authors (1-800-288-4677)

Because of the dynamic nature of the Internet, any web addresses or links contained in this book may have changed since publication and may no longer be valid. The views expressed in this work are solely those of the author and do not necessarily reflect the views of the publisher, and the publisher hereby disclaims any responsibility for them.

Any people depicted in stock imagery provided by Thinkstock are models, and such images are being used for illustrative purposes only. Certain stock imagery © Thinkstock.

ISBN: 978-1-4917-2929-8 (sc)
ISBN: 978-1-4917-2931-1 (hc)
ISBN: 978-1-4917-2930-4 (e)

Library of Congress Control Number: 2014905299

Printed in the United States of America.

iUniverse rev. date: 04/07/2014

CONTENTS

FOREWORD

Ramblings, Rants, and Ravings of a Man
As Viewed and Lived Through the Eyes of a Guy

For those who enjoy "reality" T.V. or just keeping it real this is the book for you. This will not be mistaken for any type of literary masterpiece. To the chagrin of the Publisher I chose to leave the grammar and sentence structure as I wrote it.

To be honest I was going to put the word "Average" in front of Man for the title. Then I would have had to define average by conventional terms. So even though I didn't use it I'd like to give you my version of average. It's not being the greatest at some things or the worst at others. Yea, yea that's kind of vague but let me describe why I consider myself average. In high school and junior college I was not in the Honor's Society. However I graduated in the top 10% of my high school class (over 1000 students) and had over a 3.0 grade average in college getting my Associate's Degree in Business. Although that may seem above average the fact that I'm not mechanically inclined at all brings it down to average in my opinion. That's just how I look at it, but I didn't use it in title and probably never should have mentioned it. That's how the writing of this book is going to flow, hope you like it.

I could go deeper with other comparisons but I think you see the picture. It also gives an example of how I can ramble about something I didn't even use. Anyway I'll be over the big 60 by the time this gets published and have decided to share some of my observations and views as I've gone through life. Many of you will laugh and shake your heads having had similar experiences or views.

I plan on going through a variety of subjects and remember these are my views and experiences of them. Names have been changed to protect the innocent (in some cases) or because I just can't remember them. I did say I was fast approaching 60 when I started this book. I can't guarantee every event has every detail right, but close enough that you'll get the picture. I'm choosing the subjects for different reasons and will give them to you as they come up. You will see I'm very passionate about some things and not so much about others. The not so much category may be more important to some of you, its just part of the average thing again.

It should be noted that it took a life time for me to get here, but I started putting it to print in the fall of 2012. The living part was easier than the actual writing about it, which was somewhat surprising. For the record my last English Composition class was freshman year 1975 and the school required both 101 and 102 and yes I passed although it may not show in the context of this book. So let the mayhem begin and hopefully some insights about how some men think even if they won't admit it in public.

I'm not a sports star, movie star or in any way, shape or form famous (unless this book takes off). What you read is how I saw it and how I handled it, just like every other man has to do to get through life. I use my experiences as a base line to show how I formed views and opinions. I expect all of you to relate in one way or another. If not then you will be experiencing the insights of a truly unique man.

I'll share some personal information and views about me in the "About the Author" section. Don't expect it to be conventional as most men aren't especially me. Like I told my wife during courtship, "what you see is pretty much what you get". I made that statement to every woman I ever dated and she was the only one to stick around. You can talk to her about that decision, believe me our friends have.

I'm a man/guy and I have rules and can be outright rude at times. The rules aren't numbered or written down, but the wife and daughters know them. Nothing crazy, for instance Wednesday is "pasta" day and that's what I expect to eat for supper. Serve me anything else and I will remind you of the rule as will my family. Even if you don't know me I will tell you it's pasta on Wednesday if you try to serve me anything else on that day. It doesn't mean I won't eat anything else, but pasta is the "rule".

Life has no blue print or instruction book; it's a wild ride, hang on and try to enjoy it as you go along. Here's a few of my ups and downs along that ride that I feel you will relate too and hopefully feel better about. If nothing else you can have a few laughs at my expense.

I'll start with a subject that affects most of us from the age of 17. As young teenagers we can't wait, as parents we dread, the rest just tolerate. Hope you enjoy.

1

DRIVING THE ROAD TO RAGE

I can hear those grunts from the older readers. The parents are shaking their heads sideways and any young people are shaking theirs up and down. As teenagers many of us couldn't wait to get their license and start driving. Borrowing dad's car, picking up some friends and just riding around, destination no-where, weren't those the "good old days". Not to mention the whole dating thing where you can actually pick the girl up without an escort. The father of the girl's nightmare, but the excitement of having some freedom of being on your own was incredible. It's these combinations of feelings that truly make life what it is for many of us.

Back to the driving thing, what has happened to the use of a directional or a hand signal (old school) to let your fellow drivers know your intentions? Not being clairvoyant puts me at a big disadvantage if the drivers around me don't signal for their turns. Not to sound petty, but not only would I appreciate a signal, but I would like you to turn in the direction you signal. You know what I'm talking about, those drivers who signal for a right turn then go straight or worse try to take a left. The left signal on then going right isn't acceptable either. It's amazing how so many drivers have forgotten, stopped using, or are too busy talking on their cell phones to make a turn signal.

I've been driving for around 40 years now and have seen most anything that can happen on the road. The bumper to bumper traffic due to construction or an unfortunate accident that takes hours to get through and all you can do is sit there and wait until you pass the problem and the road opens back up. Ice, snow, sleet, high winds and whatever else the weather has thrown our way I've had to drive in it. Just like the mailman sometimes you just have to go some where (usually work) no matter what the weather.

Oh lets not forget that memorable morning when I was getting onto the highway and there had been a horrendous accident. Only one lane was opened and as I passed by I witnessed a couple of the rescuer's putting someone in a body bag. It was a ghastly sight and if I had eaten breakfast that morning I probably would have lost it. As it was, I found myself shaking a bit as I continued down the road. Life is precious and seeing it taken away like that leaves a mark.

My point is I've done my share of driving and feel I can make some semi unbiased observations. For instance I have a theory that the root of road rage could be those drivers not signaling for turns. I know that's a huge leap but think about how many times you see a fellow driver not signal a turn and upset another driver, maybe even you. You can usually recognize these situations by horns blearing, a lot of yelling with some colorful language (swearing) and of course the universally known gesture of flipping the bird (giving the middle finger). Or as my daughters refer to it, flipping off or being flipped off. If the person flipping the bird is pumping it up and down or doing the double flip with both hands, then you know they are truly pissed off.

Who's to say that this type of behavior doesn't build up and fester until finally someone snap's. Let's face it there are some drivers out there that seem to be clueless or too busy gabbing on their cell phones to actually pay attention to how their driving is effecting the drivers around them. Having a driver's license is a privilege not a right (a police officer told me that once), so show a little courtesy to your fellow drivers and use your directional.

This signaling thing applies to the highway as well. Putting your blinker on to signal changing lanes is the proper way to do it. However that doesn't apply when you put your blinker on then CUT ME OFF or another driver. I use capital letters for all you texters and computer geeks so that you can hear me YELLING. Again remember you're not alone out there, look around there's plenty of other drivers on those roads. Be courteous; signal your lane changes, let fellow drivers know your intentions. It helps avoid accidents and may actually save lives including yours.

Hopefully I'm making my point, to further drive it home and help prove my road rage theory here's a series of events that happened to me on my way home from work. It was a nice spring day, warm enough to drive with the windows open. The time was mid afternoon and it had been an uneventful 8 hour shift at work. I was approaching my first four way traffic light on my route home and my light was red. There was room for two lanes, thus the cars on the left could make a left turn or go straight. Leaving the cars on right to take a right turn or possibly go straight. A normal situation and there were several cars on the other side of the street that would be coming our way also stopped at the light. Just a normal intersection we all encounter during our daily drives.

Let me further describe the situation by stating that there were three cars on the left side of the road in front of me, none of which were signaling for a left turn. Knowing this light as I did I was sure at least one of them would take the left even though they weren't signaling for it. Thus I pulled to the right side of the road and had two cars in front of me. The car directly in front of me was signaling for a right turn. The car in front of him had already started to make the turn to the right, but had no blinker on. There were three cars on the other side of the road that would be coming our way when the light changed and the front car was signaling for a left turn. Thus he was coming across traffic in my direction.

Nothing out of the ordinary, so here's what I thought would happen when the light changed. The two cars in front of me would take their right turns, while that was happening, the three cars on my left would go across the intersection. If I was right one of them would end up taking the left allowing the car coming the other way to make his left. I intended on letting him make his turn in front of me then I would continue on straight across the intersection. I would deal with any of the cars on my left that went straight as well on the other side of intersection. Again it was a situation that happens all the time at this intersection.

I had already prepared myself for someone on my left taking an unscheduled or late signaled left turn. As it happened the front car started to take the left turn, thus opening the way for the car on opposite side of the road to make his left turn as well, let the chaos begin. Then we witnessed the first boneheaded move of the lead car in my lane. As I said, this vehicle had already started to make the right hand turn even though he hadn't signaled for it. He stopped and turned left back into the intersection and almost had a head on collision with the car turning from the opposite way.

Let the mayhem continue, both drivers were yelling out there windows. Some colorful language I might add. They were beeping their horns and as the vehicle in my lane made his way around the on coming car that he had almost hit head on they exchanged some bird flipping, then he went straight across the intersection. The car in front of me let the oncoming car make his turn then he followed him. The car making the left without a signal was still sitting in the intersection so I went on my way, straight.

Yes, I am now behind the vehicle that caused the whole situation. I could see his arms flailing up in the air as he continued down the road so I gave him plenty of space. Next we come to a 4 way stop sign. As luck would have it there were no cars at the other three stop signs. Since I have already referred to the driver in front of me as making a boneheaded move I will dub him bonehead for further references. He had no signal on but took a left turn, on the bright side he did come to a complete stop first. I signaled for a left turn, stopped and continued on behind him continuing to leave plenty of space between our vehicles.

Next another 4 way stop sign where bonehead stopped and then went straight. Again after I stopped I too went straight. Trust me I was giving this guy some space. The next stop sign was a simple decision, you could go left or right. My boy stopped then took a right, no blinker. At this point I figured he was heading to the highway just like me. I continued on behind him to the next stop sign where the choices were left or straight (which was a dead end). Thus even though he didn't use a signal I knew he was going left and he did.

As we approached the set of lights that led us to the highway the bonehead went into the left hand lane. To me that meant he was taking a left or going straight. I didn't care I was sliding into the right lane and signaling for a right turn. I was almost next to the bonehead when the light changed at which time he swung into my lane almost hitting me and definitely CUTTING ME OFF, yes now I was yelling. He never even looked just turned into the lane. I hit the horn to let him know I was there and that he had just cut me off and he was kind enough to flip me the bird. I had to hand it to him he was in a world of his own and seemed to be clueless.

Yes he turned onto the on ramp just like I was doing heading onto the highway. He hadn't signaled for one turn, almost caused a head on collision and had almost gotten me in an accident. I couldn't wait to get on the highway and get away from this turkey, sorry bonehead.

I would like to say he drove off and all was well, but that wasn't the case. He literally cut across all three lanes causing several drivers to hit their breaks and honk their horns. The poor driver in the left hand lane had to lock up his breaks and go into a skid to avoid rear ending the bonehead. Apparently this was a breaking point for that driver as once he got control of his car again he started chasing the bonehead down the highway. I had to just shake my head as the two of them were bobbing in and out of traffic, even going into the breakdown lane at one point. This continued as they drove out of my sight.

It was one of those times you wished a State Trooper was around to pull them over and stop the reckless driving. I continued down the highway around 10 miles when I noticed cars were starting to break and slow down up ahead. My first thought was an accident and I had a good guess how it would have happened. Then I saw the flashing blue lights well ahead in the breakdown lane. Hoping that he had the bonehead and his pursuer pulled over I signaled my way over to the right lane for a bird's eye view. Yes a childish move, but I couldn't help it.

To my delight there were the two of them, out of their cars yelling and pointing at each other. The Trooper in between them was trying to settle the situation down. I have to admit I slowed way down and had a huge smile on my face as I passed them by. I was hoping the bonehead would look my way and see me smiling and remember cutting me off. It didn't happen, but I felt like justice was being served. I had no idea how much the Trooper had seen of how they were driving but I was hoping he caught it all.

As I continued down the road I was pondering just what those tickets were going to look like for both drivers. Speeding, driving to endanger, reckless driving, driving in breakdown lane and my favorite "failure" to signal for a lane change. There are probably a few others I missed, but I knew they were facing some serious charges, not to mention road rage.

I felt a bit bad for the second driver who got sucked into the bonehead's reckless behavior. Who knows how many other drivers this guy pissed off before I got behind him at that set of lights? For me it was the lack of signaling for those turns and blatant disregard for the drivers around him. For the second driver who got totally cutoff with no signal and almost lost control of his car he just snapped. I couldn't help but wonder how many other drivers had failed to signal for turns in his journey? I know it's a stretch, but that's why the road rage thing is a theory not fact.

I'm sure most of you have had a similar type situation develop while you were driving. Hopefully you kept your cool and just watched it unfold. If the driver of the second car is reading this then now you know a few events that happened before you got sucked in. For anyone else who may have gotten sucked into a similar situation there was probably a series of events that triggered the whole thing. The moral of the story is being courteous to your fellow drivers and of course signal for your turns.

Obviously there is a lot more to driving than the use of turn signals. Traffic lights, stop and yield signs, speed limits and the list goes on. With the exception of the speed limit being violated the lack of signaling for turns is right up there with most violations. It's also a pet peeve of mine in case you hadn't notice. I think I made my point so let's move on to parking.

NO PARKING signs mean NO PARKING, yes I'm yelling again. It doesn't get any simpler, no means no. Again not to sound petty but waiting in the car while someone runs into a store for a quick item doesn't change the meaning of the sign. That goes for you the driver running in as well. The NO is for everyone. When there are other exceptions like FIRE LANE they are clearly noted. You're not special; you should park in the designated area for your vehicle.

That goes for designated handicapped spaces as well. Unless you have a handicap placard like myself stay out of those spaces. Trust me they serve a purpose for those of us that need them.

Along the same lines we are seeing more and more designated spaces for expecting mothers. Not to be rude, but just because you may be an overweight woman who may look pregnant doesn't qualify. I'm sure I'll be getting some hate mail for that statement, but seriously, the signs are there to help the people, who need them, find another spot.

By the way most parking areas or lots have painted lines to designate where you can park your cars. The lines are spaced so that you can park your vehicle between them, not in the middle of them or across them. They are there to keep the parking uniform and in most cases maximize the spaces available. When someone doesn't park between the lines it usually starts a chain reaction with the next car unable to get between the lines. I'm not writing in a foreign language here, I would like to think you all know what I'm eluding too.

My family thinks I tend to be a little anal about things, but honestly sometimes you follow the rules to be courteous to the people around you. What a novel concept actually considering another person or being courteous. I must be some kind of rebel to think this way, lock me up and throw away the key.

I'm not going to bore you with any parking lot stories, just go to the store and look around. I'm guessing you will see some type of parking violation, probably more than one. The bigger the parking lots (like a shopping mall) the more violations. They tend to be so blatant and unnecessary you almost expect to see them. If you happen to be one of these offenders, again think of your fellow parkers. Who knows it might catch on, doing the right thing, following the rules, what a concept?

To wrap up this subject let me leave you with a fun little game I play when driving on short trips. It tracks how many vehicles are properly using their directionals. It's real simple; if a driver signals for a turn and takes it you add 1 point, when the driver doesn't signal for a turn that they take it -1 point. If they signal for a turn and then don't take it -1 point. As a bonus for a real bonehead move its -2 for signaling for one turn and then taking another. I only count the vehicles affecting my trip.

The point unfortunately is more often than not your going to end your trip in negative numbers. The higher the negative the less courteous your fellow drivers tend to be. I live in Southeastern Mass. and my fellow drivers fail on a regular basis.

There you have my first chapter, if you liked it then hopefully you will enjoy the other subjects to follow. Like the title suggests this is how I see it right, wrong or some cases aggravating and hopefully with a little added humor. No matter how serious a subject is I always try to find some humor. It drives my wife crazy, but she's stuck around for over 34 years.

I need to sneak in an audible here, as while I was just driving to the Dentist I realized I missed two important aspects regarding driving. The first is seatbelts, without them you probably would not be reading this book. Hopefully that's considered a positive; although it could be debated depending on how mad my wife or kids are with me.

When I was growing up seatbelts weren't even in cars yet, nor car seats for infants and young children. Back in my youth we would ride in the back bed of pickup trucks. Today that would be considered a hanging offense for the driver if caught.

I did not embrace seatbelts when they were first introduced to the automobile. It wasn't until my wife and I started a family that brought the importance to my attention. We were strapping our first child in so it made sense for us to buckle up as well. It also helped later in life when we forced the practice onto our children. Since we were already using them it prevented one of those awkward and some what hypocritical moments of do as I say not what I do. We were setting it up by example.

Without boring you with the details I can attest to the fact that the seatbelt saved my life. I had the misfortune of being in a multi-car accident on the highway. When I regained conscience my car was off the road and the windshield was smashed along with the rest of the car. There I was strapped in by my seatbelt. I suffered a separated shoulder and a nasty concussion, but I was able to unhook my seatbelt and walk away.

Unfortunately, I would find out later that other members of the accident who weren't wearing seatbelts didn't survive the accident. The State Trooper told me that my seatbelt had probably saved my life. Now the first thing I do when I enter a vehicle whether as the driver or passenger is fasten that seatbelt. Now it's the law and one I never break. I can also report that both my daughters have been in minor accidents and were wearing their seatbelts. A lesson well learned that makes their mother and me very proud.

Next item I forgot to mention is wearing a helmet when riding on a motorcycle. I don't ride, but with the amount of bad drivers out there it makes a lot of sense. It's not a nation wide law yet but it probably should be. I'm not going to debate the different views of this safety feature, just make a point. Chances are if you are knocked off or thrown from a motorcycle you will hit your head at some point. If nothing else the helmet will help keep your face and head from looking like mince meat.

To make the point a little stronger most people riding bicycles wear helmets and definitely make their children wear them. They go a lot slower than motorcycles, but it's somewhat the same principle.

Another large problem that has developed with drivers is the use of their cell phones, especially TEXTING, again with the yelling. I'm sure most of you have seen drivers cross into lanes or almost hit someone head on because they were using their phone in some manner. Texting has become the biggest culprit as of late.

There really is a good deterrent to this behavior and that is to treat texting offenders the same way as drivers under the influence. The problem it creates is similar to drinking; it impedes our driving and slows the reaction time because people aren't paying attention to the road.

I know it's harsh but the death toll is growing at an alarming rate from drivers more interested in their phone than the road. From my point of view if you have a loved one hurt or killed in a car accident because the other driver was just texting you're not going to feel any better than if they had been drinking.

Sadly the other day a woman caused an accident because she was allegedly texting that she was driving under the influence. This one is wrong on several levels and I will leave it at that. Make the penalty harsh so people understand how important the issue is concerning what you do when driving, just my opinion.

I know there is a lot more to the subject of driving, but those are the highlights for me at the present time, next chapter please.

2

LOVE, SEX, and MARRIAGE

You can arrange the words describing this chapter in whatever order that fits your relationship. None of my sex first relationships worked out. When I met my wife Cynthia we fell in love, which lead to a sexual relationship culminating in marriage. I'm comfortable mentioning sex in second position as both my in-laws are no longer with us. They were two of the nicest people you could ever meet, but they were old school Italians. My mother-in-law Mary was one of the sweetest women I ever met. A great cook and very family first orientated. She and Phil (my father-in-law), went to church every week when healthy and had a strong religious and moral background. They may have known about the sex, but they didn't need it confirmed. I'm guessing most parents are like that, I know I am with my two daughters.

It was their strong family values and loving marriage that reinforced the idea of marriage for me. I'm sure I wasn't their first choice for a son-in-law, but they always made me feel welcome. Marriage is a tough long haul and having supportive in-laws really helped.

I've been married for over 34 years to my wife Cynthia. Many say it's because she is a Saint and she is quick to agree. Most wives will probably make that statement about their marriages as well. We've had our ups and downs like all couples, but have always been able to work out our differences. With the divorce rate somewhere near the 50% mark these days I think it's our love for each other that has carried us through the tough times. That is why Love comes first for me and hopefully my family. Cynthia is always reminding our daughters that her love for me is how she got through the tough times. I like to add a few terms like "salt of the earth, nice guy, meal ticket and of course great in bed" which always gets the "dad too much info" and "that's just wrong" comments from the daughters.

Yes I'm one of those parents who enjoys embarrassing my kids every chance I get. For those of you who have daughters over the age of 21 and they are still dating feel free to use a line from the movie "Bird on a Wire" regarding their male choices. Asking "can he throw the leg?" gets a great response from my daughters, which they tell me, is one of the reasons they have daddy issues. I just think it's funny and Cynthia gets a kick out of it as well. Like my tee shirt says "don't take life so seriously, it isn't permanent". Anyway back to the subject.

I'm no marital expert, but I'm guessing Sex becomes an integral part of a good relationship. It brings two people even closer together. I'm not even going to try and explain it, but for my wife and me our love just seemed to get stronger with our sexual connection. From there marriage was a given.

Honestly it just feels like a strong three step process. Marriage is a work in progress; skip either of the first two steps and you're probably going into the 50% divorce category.

So that's the vanilla part of the chapter and a nice black and white start. However nothing is ever just black and white. So let's go back in time a bit to the late 60's and early 70's when I was a teenager.

In those days if a young man got a young woman pregnant they got married. It was abruptly thought of as a shot gun wedding. Even back then I thought this was a bad idea and the guns were imaginary in the few I attended. To date I have no friends or relatives that got married under those circumstances and are still married. Be it a small sample, it's still a statistic in my life experiences. Just my opinion but the pregnant thing in some cases doesn't allow the Love/Sex steps to really develop and grow. The couple goes right into family mode and they miss what was a great time of growing as a couple. As my wife puts it we aren't just a couple we are best friends.

Interracial dating never mind marriage were not acceptable behavior. There were cultures/ nationalities that frowned on marrying outsiders. There were still many families where the grand parents came over from Europe and did not look kindly on mixed marriages. No kidding and I will give you two examples just from my group of friends.

My best friend, who was also my best man at my wedding, was from Irish descent. He was dating a young woman of Jewish persuasion. When she brought him home to meet the parents all you know what broke out. Her father demanded she stop dating him because he wasn't Jewish. Another friend had a similar situation with the father of a Greek woman he was dating.

You get the picture that interracial, mixed religions and mixed nationalities were considered radical marriages or relationships at that time. That being said these marriages when they occurred were recognized as valid unions. Even then there were stipulations as far as religions went.

For instance I was brought up Protestant and my wife Catholic, to be married in a Catholic church we had to agree to raise any children we had as Catholics. It was a non-negotiable issue if you were to be married in a Catholic church. We also had to meet with the Priest for classes before we qualified as a couple to be married in the Catholic Church. Thankfully there was another couple taking the classes with us at the time. For me it was no big deal.

I was and still am very much in love with my wife and I knew both her parents were strong Catholics as well as 100% Italian descent. There was never a question on my part that I would do whatever the Church required. For the record we followed through and raised both daughters as Catholics.

The only thing I remember about those classes and discussions were the arguments about Annulments'. Not being Catholic, the thought you could just erase a marriage seemed odd to me. I remember the other couple and my wife questioning what happens to the children of those marriages.

The bottom line about these mixtures of marriages was that the government had nothing to do with them. The stipulations were imposed depending on what Church you wanted to have your wedding at. A Justice Of The Peace would have married you with none of those stipulations.

You may have guessed where this is going and that is Gay marriage. I'm no expert on the Bible or religion so if I might be mistaken on some of my next few statements, it's unintentional. To my knowledge the biggest point about marriage is that both people are in love with each other. Sorry people but when you fall in love it just happens. Color of skin, age, and yes gender should not be brushed aside, love is love and it can happen to the strangest of couples.

It may have been frowned upon to marry outside your race, religion or nationality, but they weren't banned nor need a law to allow them. Let's remember the original concept of marriage was until "death" do you part. Now we are in the 50% divorce range.

Let's face it the heterosexuals' aren't doing a great job with the concept of marriage. When I grew up I only knew of one couple that were divorced, that's right one. To take the divorce thing one step further, the process tends to get very ugly. What was supposed to start out as two people deeply in love changes very drastically? It's called the fine line between love and hate.

My point being if the heterosexual community is only getting it right 1 out of 2 times why are so many against Gay marriage. Who knows maybe they will have better luck or commitment to the concept of marriage. If not let them share with the ugliness of the divorce that goes with failed marriages. Kind of the misery likes company concept for those who have the misfortune of getting divorced.

If I recall my History, our forefathers came to this Country to have such freedoms. Not to sound too radical here, but if we aren't allowing gay marriages should we revisit other mixed marriages. After all we are trying to tell people what type of person they can fall in love with, so let's clean it all up.

While we're at it let's start by getting some IQ tests involved as well. Let's set some minimal number you must meet in order to get married and have children. If love isn't going to be the main reason why two people can get married then I say clean it up all together. Go for it and clean up the Gene pools.

Hopefully you understand how absurd I'm starting to sound. The point of a marriage between two people should be love, no matter what the mix happens to be.

Hopefully I haven't lost any readers yet so hang in there and look at things from even another angle. Since the divorce rate is so high many of them remarry. This creates another dynamic for any children of the first marriage, two dads or two moms or both. Granted the new parent is tagged Step parent, but you can see a similar situation for the child as having the same sex parents. The Step parent is supposed to except and Love the family he or she marries into. The biggest difference is sex.

I have some news for all you parents out there, your kids don't want to know or think about your sex lives with your partners. That being said throw in the fact of the sex being in the privacy of the bedroom and what matters to the child is the love within the family. There's that key word Love again.

Gay couples tend to adopt children who do not have parents or homes to live at and give them that loving family. So let's wake up and smell that free air that Americans are so proud of and let two people who fall in love get married.

If not I say again, lets clean it up all together. That's right, keep those gene pools pure. In this world there would be no interracial marriages. No marriages outside the religion or nationality. Why stop there, institute the IQ test and limit people within 20 points of each other compatible to marry. Let's add body types to that list, tall with tall, short with short, skinny with skinny and so on.

How far should we take this, hair and eye color the same. Let's not forget Class, after all that's how they breed horses. How about we throw in looks, which would eliminate any more Julie Roberts/ Lyle Lovett type marriages, I mean how blind is love? Lyle what were you thinking?

Again hopefully you're seeing how absurd things could get. I'm guessing there might be fewer marriages and more people living together. Not sure what that does to the family value concept or religion within family.

If I'm totally off base and it's the sex that has people at arms with gay marriage, well that's none of their business. I'm certainly not opening my bedroom doors for all to see. There are still religions and cultures that feel the missionary position is the one and only way two people should make love, and then only for the purpose of making babies. Just a guess but if the missionary position is the only one in your marriage you're heading for divorce or infidelity.

Enough, I stand by my original concept, Love, Sex, and then Marriage, when you're ready. I don't care the mixture as long as they are in love and happy. I can't say I was happy with all my daughters dating choices, but they have both found a loving partner and that's all that counts. Now I have 2 very mechanical minded Son-In-Laws, which comes in very handy. It's also obvious that they truly love my daughters, which is all my wife and I ever hoped for.

In the end the two people in a marriage are the ones that live together. Live and let live, if they're happy that's a great thing. Hope I didn't make it too simple for you but it actually can be that way when you fall in love. It's the mind and what you think people will think that clouds everything up. Life is too short to be unhappy and too much fun to go through it alone.

3

SPORTS JUST PART OF LIFE

Hey I'm a guy, you had to know this would be a subject I would have some views and opinions on. For starters professional athletes make way too much money for what they do. When you make more money than the President of the USA to play a sport something's out of whack.

I blame the owner's mostly, but we the fans have to take some of that blame as well. The player's have agents that negotiate the best and highest paid contracts they can get for their players. I compare it to a Union that negotiates a contract for its members. Unlike companies that negotiate with the unions, the owners have let the pay scale get way out of hand for the sake of winning. It's literally "winning at any costs". Some of these sports have become multi-billion dollar industries so a high market owner has a lot of money to throw at players.

Here's where we the fans have to take some blame as we support these teams by purchasing the high priced tickets for games, buying team and player souvenirs, not to mention the price we pay for food and drinks at the games themselves. Yesterday someone released a new sneaker for $300; I almost fell out of my chair. I don't own any article of clothing that I paid over $100 for including a winter coat. Are we hitting the ridiculous point yet?

Personally I have not attended a game for many years for a variety of reasons. One is the price of tickets, but another is how every major sport has gone on strike or been locked out by the owners over money. The fans are the ones who should be on strike and boycotting games until ticket prices come way down. It costs a family of 4 over $200 to go to sporting event. That could buy a couple weeks groceries for that same family.

That $200 just covers seats, not parking, food and beverage and I'm probably low balling that amount. The last event I brought my family to was when the Fleet Center opened and I brought them to a Celtics game mid season. To give my two daughters the same experience I had going to games I even brought them to the game via Public Transportation, the MBTA. I bought mid priced tickets, 24 rows up so I exceeded the $200 limit with that and the transportation. The food and beverages were also higher than usual as they both developed appetites of small gorillas once at the game.

Let's not forget the TV revenue these leagues and teams get for televising regular season and playoff games. The stations bid against themselves to make those revenues astronomical as well. That's why ESPN has so many channels. I pay for it in my cable bill, which my wife thinks is crazy. However I pay less money in a year for ESPN than I would by going to just one game and no crowds.

Since I'm mentioning ESPN let me go off on a little tangent here and tell you the charitable suggestion I made via e-mail to their website. Since they have so many stations and viewers that they reach, especially male of nature, I suggested a Calendar. Lets face it they have some of the most knowledgeable and beautiful women sportscasters. My suggestion was a tasteful Calendar depicting the women of ESPN in their ESPN daily attire for charity. Let the ladies chose their charities and divide the proceeds accordingly. As I stated in my e-mail please put me down for one. I know this was way off beat, but I thought it was a great idea, firemen do it. You see more and more of these women on commercials. Why not a nonprofit calendar with proceeds going to charity? They would probably have fun with it.

Let's get back to sports and drop the money situation as we the fan will really never have much control over it. Like it or not people and corporations will pay for tickets. So let me continue by saying my friends and I grew up playing all different sports depending on the season.

We played baseball during the spring and summer, football in fall, basketball and street hockey in winter. I actually played soccer in junior high so add that to the fall schedule when we had enough kids to play. None of us played those sports for a High School team, but we still had fun and made what we felt were some great plays. I'm sure we all had that game or games they remember for different reasons. Those were fun times, great exercise and a lot of laughs. Playing the different sports gave you much more of an insight into them.

One of my friends new the bus and train schedules going from our suburban town into Boston and we used to go to games at Boston Garden. Back then we could see the Celtics or Bruins during the week for around $10. That included ticket, transportation and a Hot Dog and drink. The Celtics were a dynasty back then. One time we even went to see Bruno Samartino wrestle, he was the champ back then. Obviously it was a different time back then.

One of the points I'm trying to make about Sports is growing up they were a big part of my life even though I wasn't one of the better players. We all played no matter what skill level you were at and the object was to have fun. We went to school, came home, went out and played some type of sport, then home for supper. It's how we grew up.

I was lucky enough to grow up in the suburbs of Boston, so I was able to witness some great teams and players. In the late 50's and 60's the Boston Celtics were a dynasty. They won 9 championships in 11 years. Carl "Yaz" hit for the Triple Crown in baseball, the last player to do so until 2012. Bobby Orr led the Bruins to a Stanley Cup in hockey. I actually have an autographed picture of him leaving his skates to score a big goal. It was compliments of my wife making some window treatments for one of his homes. The Bruins won another Cup recently as well.

In the 80's we had the Larry Bird era for the Celtics and a couple more championships. They had a great rivalry with the Lakers and Magic Johnson back then. The New England Patriots got slammed by the Bears in a Superbowl. Now the Patriots seem to be competing for Superbowls every year. They've won 3 and lost a couple during that time. I get to see one of the best quarterbacks in the game in Tom Brady.

Lastly we have the Red Sox who have won 2 World Series and have been playoff contenders annually until there epic collapse in 2011. Sadly, the organization handled the collapse as so many do. It was a player collapse and some poor actions and judgments by some of those players during their off days.

So ownership let their Players Manager Terry Francona go along with the GM Theo Epstein. Arguably they were responsible for those 2 championships. They lost there All-Star closer to free agency, he appeared to take the first offer to get out of town. All the players whose names were thrown around for their poor judgments during the collapse stayed. Just being a fan you aren't privy to the private conversations behind closed doors, but something seemed very wrong to me the fan.

The strangeness continued when several players were talked to about who would be the replacement manager. The one man they were told would not be hired was, Bobby Valentine and then that's who they hired. He criticized one of their better players, Kevin Youkillis, which ruffled some feathers. It caused another player to bring up that criticizing players in public was not the Boston way. It was obvious right then that the chemistry of the team just wasn't there and the season had just started. 2012 was supposed to be a better year, not the collapse that happened.

Then a story leaked saying it was Youk who told management about what was going on in the clubhouse on those players off days. I must admit I was never a big fan of Youk and he was having a bad year. His back up was outplaying him so it was no surprise when he was traded to the White Sox. Since the trade Youk is playing much better and the White Sox are leading in their division. The Red Sox however have gone further downhill. Not to mention the backup Millbrook got hurt shortly after the move.

Call it karma but the so called problem players were still on the team until yesterday. Things worked out nicely for me since I was writing this chapter when the Red Sox and Dodgers have made one of the biggest trades in baseball history. The Red Sox traded their best every day player in Adrian Gonzales (who wasn't putting up the numbers they thought he would when they got him). Throw in Carl Crawford who was a total bust and oft injured and way over paid. Then there was Josh Beckett who appeared to me as a prima donna who just didn't get it. Again his pitching seemed to be going downhill fast with a questionable work ethic. He was one of the players mentioned in those off day incidents as well. Lastly a nice bench player in Nick Punto of whom I know little about and seemed to be doing his job.

In return we got the Dodger's slumping first baseman (who's a free agent after this year), to take Gonzales place and a few young prospects. The positive news for Red Sox fans according to management was the huge salary relief of $250 million dollars (that's a lot of money) and purging several players that no longer seemed to fit in the Red Sox plans or ways of doing things. Myself several of those players should have been gone after last years collapse. Now we will see how the new GM can rebuild the team and how quickly, as Boston fans aren't very patient.

All those players went to teams that will be going to the playoffs. It wouldn't be a total surprise to me if the White Sox play the Dodgers in the World Series. (It actually was the Giants and Tigers with the Giants winning). Talk about falling in horse manure and coming up smelling like a rose. My point is if I was a die heart Boston sports fan then I would have my fair share of titles and high points.

The 2012 football season is about to open with "replacement" officials, are you kidding me (they lasted through the 3rd week as I recall). A multibillion dollar business and you don't want to pay your officials. Yes they make mistakes, but from what I've seen in preseason they are 10 times better than what I've seen from the replacements. We'll see how the players and owners react when blown calls start to cost teams' potential game winning situations. I usually don't watch preseason football, but I wanted to see how bad the officiating might be. I'm guessing those people betting the games will be concerned as well. It was after the Green Bay/Seattle game in Week 3 when the officials were brought back. It took a brutal call and public outrage but it happened.

I love football, especially college games, as these players are giving it 100% all the time. If they don't the coaches will sit them down no matter what their star status happens to be. Of course that's because the coaches get paid big bucks and the players get none. That's a big controversy because of all the revenue the colleges get from their football programs.

Let's not forget that these players have an opportunity of getting a first class education and pay nothing if they are scholarship players. You're talking about $100,000 or more educations to prepare them for life after college. Many non athletic students with much stronger academic resumes would love to have those opportunities. Most students now days leave college with some hefty student loans to pay off. Scholarship athletes just walk away with an education and possible pro career.

I know it's not as simple as I put it, but I'm not far off the reality. A friend's daughter went to law school and has a huge student loan debt. Becoming a lawyer is no small feat, but it came at a price. Today's star college athletes' leave school early and don't get degrees. Others get general degrees that may not be that helpful when they do graduate.

My point is the education should be the focal point not the athletic performance. That's why most of the Pro- sports other than football take young athletes right out of high school. I hate to burst the bubble but some young people are not college material. Pro football forces them to do just that, so I'm not surprised when some of them have academic problems and questionable class loads.

Final point on the subject is the student athlete should take advantage of the opportunity they get for the education, which is what over 90% of the college students are there for.

I'm also tired of the athletes in general getting preferential treatment. This off season in football alone they had players get arrested more than once with little to no penalties. If a normal guy got arrested for DUI then a few months later drug possession or driving with a suspended license he would be facing some serious probation and counseling time, possibly even some jail time. Their life would definitely take some serious changes, not to mention the fines.

These athletes apologize with some questionable reasons and go back to their million dollar careers. In real life some of these offenses would cost people their jobs. The first offense would have been a warning, the second and you're gone in many cases, but not pro sports.

Let's take this a step forward with the drug policies. Joe or Jill average American fails a drug test at their job and they are fired. In most sports it's a warning or small suspension. The second offense is a longer suspension, but you still have a job once it's served.

It's time we take the pro athlete off their pedestal and treat them like every one else. They make outrageous money and get more than their share of breaks and opportunities. Enough said.

Just a couple predictions for the upcoming 2012 season, Alabama repeats as college champs (I was right). I like a great team in college football who has their starting Quarterback coming back the next season. It wouldn't surprise me if Ravens play the Packers in the Superbowl with the Pack winning (It was Ravens beating 49er's) not bad predictions.

I went through an interesting move about 4 months ago, not to mention the prepacking time and POD the wife and I filled. Needless to say I stopped writing in late November and I'm starting back up mid-March. No we're not settled into our newly purchased home. Anyway that is why I added some updates in () regarding my picks in playoffs.

Alabama was an easy pick, but Ravens were a nice pick. The Packers really let me down. As for the baseball picks, better luck next year, maybe Dodgers- Angels will be in the World Series for 2013.

March Madness is now upon us I have Duke playing Kansas for the title (Louisville beat Michigan). There are some great Prop bets out in Vegas. It's a bit like Superbowl where you can bet multiple non game bets. A couple I like are the Big 10 winning more than 13 games combined (won), all the #2 Seeds to win more than 9 games (lost). How about a #2 Seed winning it all for a $100 bet if you get $450 back (lost). I honestly think if Duke doesn't win both Ohio St and Miami of Fla. have great chances. Yes I was way off.

Oh yes I forgot to mention that hockey was locked out to start the season. Like me not a lot of people cared just the players and a few die heart fans. It was funny during the football lockout and basketball lockout it was all ESPN ever talked about. They spent hours each day discussing the possibilities in nauseam. Then when hockey did it there was barely a mention. Check out the ESPN website sometimes NHL isn't even listed as a top line sport on their header. Yet once again they argued over money at the expense of the fan. The Blackhawks beat the Bruins for the Stanley Cup in the shortened season.

As I stated earlier it just makes no sense to me. If these owners feel that their sports are a business then run it accordingly and let the chips fall like a normal business. Actually make both parties live up to and abide by contracts they signed. No player holdouts live by the same work rules the normal worker has too live by. You don't go to work or are a no call no show you are terminated. Insubordination is a terminating offense as well.

Criminal behavior, poor performance, drug use, sexual harassment and the list goes on are reasons for termination. No benefits or buyouts your gone end of story.

Hello, professional athletes the real world can be harsh. Likewise for owners who shall we say try to protect their players with preferential treatment. It's amazing what some of these players get away with and are tolerated by their owners because they are a good or key player. I'm not sure either party wants to live and operate under true business rules and regulations.

Let me revisit this chapter at this time as the Master's golf tournament is going on. Tiger Woods was just penalized for a

2 stroke penalty for not dropping his ball properly after having his previous shot hit the flag and go into the water. I think what this guy has done and may do on the golf course is incredible. This offense could have cost him a disqualification so it was a pretty serious offense. My thought/question is where was the official who was probably close by following this group? It took a replay and overnight complaint to bring about the penalty. I'm not sure there are many other sports that access a penalty the next day for an infraction. Looking back it sure would fix some blown calls.

I played golf for a few years (not very well) so I know there are all sorts of rules regarding where you ball lands when it's not in play. That being said the official could have stepped up here and reviewed his options, after all it's one of the reasons they are out there isn't it?

The other tough ruling was the 1 stroke penalty the 14 year old amateur got for slow play after a warning. I understand the letter of the law but where talking a kid with a lot of pressure on him. Heck rules are rules just glad he still made the cut.

So remember 4-12-13 as a very tough day in sports. My wife always says things tend to happen in threes with certain things and it did yesterday in sports. First the above 14 year old became the youngest player to make the cut for the weekend play in the Master's despite the penalty. On the same day the #1 player, Tiger got a 2 stroke penalty the next morning for an illegal drop, that same day. Lastly in basketball Kobe Bryant suffered a season ending Achilles injury that will require surgery. Rehab could be 6 to 9 months. Looks like tough times for those LA Lakers.

This probably isn't relevant but an old friend used to joke "rehab was for quitters". I know sick humor, but I have a teeshirt with that saying on it. Anyway Adam Scott won the Masters with a nice birdie putt on the 2nd playoff hole. He came from 3 back and I must admit I have been a fan of his since he hired Tiger's old caddie.

Many people don't get the allure of golf and I was one of them. When I started to play I was terrible and just didn't get it. Trust me it's much harder than it looks on TV. The thing about golf isn't just the game it's the majesty of the courses you play. You're outdoors with trees, flowers, birds and occasionally a few animals. Personally I have seen deer, coyotes and the usual local animals on a course.

On one morning there was a hawk perched on a branch overlooking a fairway we were playing. What brought him to our attention was when he swooped down and grabbed my ball off the fairway and flew off with it. It was the second time wildlife had interfered with one of my shots. A few years earlier a muskrat came out of a pond and pushed my ball into the water. I was playing with a friend and his father-in-law and they got quite the laugh.

For those who play the game you know that crazy things can happen to your ball out on the course and I'm sure many have stories to share. Let me share a couple of mine at this time. Please keep the laughter to a minimum. My friends who witnessed them will definitely remember and get a chuckle. Feel free to add the words "stop me if you heard this or it happened to you" on the golf course.

I was a terrible golfer and for years could not break the 100 stroke barrier. As I said it's tougher than it looks. Anyway one fine sunny day a few of us took the day off from work and traveled to a course I had never played. We met a few other players there who I had never met. One of those men was legally blind, no joke here, he could only see a few feet in front of himself. His playing partner would spot him over his ball and describe his situation and distance from flag. It was a little more involved than that but hopefully you get the picture.

That day I played in his group. It was amazing how well and straight he could hit the ball. I would learn later he was a good golfer before losing his eyesight. As we took the turn after 9 holes he was beating me which my fellow golfers were enjoying and rubbing it in a bit. Even he pointed out that I was losing to a "blind guy". However I was at 48 for the 9 holes which meant I had a good chance to break the magic 100.

Needless to say I was the brunt of more than a few jokes, but everyone was really having a good time. What helped for me was the fact I was playing my best round to date. As we stood on the 18th tee my score was 92 and the hole was a par 4 dogleg left. Of course my tee shot went a bit wide and in the rough, but playable. A nice recovery shot back on the fairway and my next shot landed on the green about 10 feet from the hole. I two putted for a 97 and the magic 100 had been broken.

I would like to say it was good enough to beat the blind guy, but it wasn't. All the ribbing I got from everyone including him didn't matter I shot a 97. I knew then it was only a matter of a few rounds before I would do it on our home course. I was right, a couple weeks later I shot a 98. After that I was shooting in the high 90's the rest of the season.

Happily the good golf continued for a few years and I was actually scoring in the low 90's here and there. Yes breaking 90 on the home course was the new goal. It only happened once, but what a great story it turned out to be, for me anyway.

We were standing on the 14th tee and I had been hitting the ball well. It looked like another low 90 was coming my way. It was a par 5 and my tee shot turned out to be my best and longest of the day. I had learned that my best shot was from about 100 yards out from the green and that had become my goal on the par 4 and par 5 holes. Yes my next shot got me to my goal and I chipped it up on the green just a few feet from the hole. I walked onto the green and tapped in my birdie putt like it was nothing. Those who play know that this can really get the adrenalin flowing.

Next hole was a par 4 and I nailed another great tee shot to the 100 yard area. Casually walked up and knocked another shot close to the cup. Trying not to think about it I stepped up and sank another birdie putt. Yes I was jumping up and down because I had never had two birdies in a row and could count the times I had two birdies in the same round on one hand.

On to the par three 16th hole, which was 120 yards, a hole I always seemed to play well I went excitingly up to tee off. Once again I hit a nice tee shot went to the green and two putted for my par. Over to the 17th we went. Another par 3 playing 140 yards and my adrenalin was really pumping now. I had just hit 3 of my best tee shots ever and was feeling pretty darn good about myself.

No exaggeration my next tee shot landed inches from the cup. As it rolled across the green I thought I might have the elusive Hole In One, which I never did get. Tapped in the putt for my 3rd birdie in four holes and on to the 18th we went. Trying not to think much about it I went up to the tee and hit my ball onto the fairway.

It wasn't a very good drive and I knew I couldn't reach the green from there. Thus I slapped my next shot around the 100 yard marker and hit my 3rd shot onto the green. I couldn't tell you how far I was from the hole but it was somewhere in the 20 foot range. As I looked over the putt all I was thinking was get it close so I could tap it in for my 89.

As I stood over the ball I was literally shaking, so I backed off. I can't even describe all the thoughts that were going through my head as I stood on that green. My buddies never said a word just let me regroup and waited. I had a little chuckle with myself and went back to hit the putt. As soon as I hit the ball the three of them started chanting "go in go in" and that's exactly what it did. I don't think I ever jumped so high in my life and the guys were giving quite the cheer. As I pulled my ball from the cup I realized I had just played the last 5 holes at 3 under par and had shot an 88 at my home course. A feat I would never duplicate or beat.

A great thing about golf is that all that play will have their funny stories and eventful rounds or shots that they made or witnessed. Put two strangers together and if they both play golf they could talk for hours. Crazy/interesting things tend to happen on the golf course hope mine brought some laughs.

Sadly I'm unable to play golf any more, but I still have some great memories. I played with a great group of guys and I'm sure they remember some of the wacky things that happened to me on the course. No kidding I actually chipped a ball up in the air and it landed behind me without hitting anything. You can't make that stuff up.

We had some great times out there and at times laughed so hard tears would fill your eyes. If nothing else I was comic relief. I would like to think most of the people who have played have seen some of these wacky things happen and not just the ones that happened to me.

I know I'm lingering a bit on this but there really are some crazy things that happen on the golf course. Watching a guy climbing a tree to retrieve the club he threw up there after a bad shot or hitting said tree an having the ball fly behind where you hit it from.

One of my favorites is seeing someone hitting a shot at the edge of a water hazard then falling into the water. Sadly I did that twice. Or that guy who throws his golf bag, clubs and all into the pond and walks off the course (never did that one). I won't go into the things that can go wrong while being in a golf cart.

Always blame those accidents on the brakes or lack thereof, if an incident happens to you.

Let's not forget those errand balls when you hear someone yelling 4 (bad shot into people) warning them it's coming. I've scattered some people in my day. OK I'll move on now.

The baseball season of 2013 is well under way and a PED scandal is breaking wide open again. PED is "performance enhancing drugs", for those not familiar with the term. It appears that a couple former MVP's and about 20 other players may have been involved. The story broke months ago and all parties were denying everything.

It appears they now have the owner of the distribution company coming forward and spilling the beans so to speak. Early reports are the league wants to treat the players who lied about their involvement first time around as second time offenders. I doubt the players union will allow that, but you never know.

This PED thing has become a line in the sand issue in most sports especially baseball. There is a little thing known as the Baseball Hall Of Fame, which baseball writers vote to see who gets in. To date any player that has been remotely associated with PED's or steroid use has been black balled by said writers.

Since the problem is continuing the Hall could be in for a period of years with few to no players getting enough votes to get in. We're talking some of the best statistical players of my time not getting in.

I honestly don't know what the solution is to this problem as it appears the players are continuing to use these drugs. Not many weeks go by that a minor league player in baseball doesn't get a 50 game suspension for violating the drug policy. It happens less often in the majors, but it hasn't stopped.

Sadly I think the dreaded "*" will be placed beside all the players of this generation. It will note their accomplishments were during the PED era. Guilty or not they will all be grouped together.

Many of these athletes hang their reputation as not failing any drug tests, some plead the fifth. Sorry guys but the fact you didn't get caught doesn't make you innocent. The bottom line is the writers do the voting and they just don't believe many of the top players weren't as they put it "juicing".

Time will tell how this period goes down in history, but it's looking bleak now. The owners turned a blind eye on this steroid use for many years. They had the Armed Forces motto "Don't ask don't tell". Now that it's all becoming public and the use continues they act appalled.

The 2013 baseball All Star game is being played as I'm writing these comments. Winning team has home field advantage in World Series, which is absurd. Best overall record should always have advantage as they earned it in the field. Where was the player's union when this rule came into play?

I'm not a diehard purest of any sport, but the overall record should stand for something throughout the playoff system in all sports. This year the American league is loaded and may have several teams with the best overall records. Yet this All Star game could give a lesser team home field advantage in the World Series? Hope I'm not in the minority on this subject. Thankfully the AL won.

So the second half of the baseball season begins with two teams really playing some great ball right now, Tamp Bay for AL and L.A. Dodgers for NL, hope they aren't peaking to early. I have some future bets and they are all still alive. This means no key injuries have derailed my teams.

Sports in general have teams with up and down years. They may keep their core players but still underachieve from the year before. I've found that it doesn't matter what the sport is, consistent winning for a team doesn't always happen. That's why many teams make some crazy trades before their trade deadlines to help get them into the playoffs. The logic being once in playoffs anything can happen as in your team gets hot or other teams have some tough injuries.

A good example is the NY Giants in football. They have won two Superbowls recently when barely getting into the playoffs. Were they the best team or just the best and luckiest during the playoffs?

I bring this point up because last year the Washington National's had a very good team and knew they were probably going to the playoffs. They had a young strong team on both sides of the ball with some very good starting pitching. One of their starters was Strasburg who was coming off a serious Tommy John type surgery, but was pitching very well. They had him on a strict pitch count each game and wanted to limit his innings for the year. He was their ACE (best) starting pitcher was young and they wanted to protect his and the teams future.

Those sports people out there know where I'm going with this as they did a bad job managing his starts and innings so that he reached his maximum weeks before the playoffs. They stuck to their guns and made him non eligible for the playoffs. Personally, I thought they were being a bit arrogant as they felt they had a young team that would only get better and should be in the playoffs for years to come.

Sadly they are finding out what I've seen happen throughout the years over all of sports. Teams change personnel and or managers; the players have off years and tough injuries, the chemistry of team changes. Let's not forget other teams make changes and sometimes their players have great years and their chemistry just clicks.

Having the highest payroll or the best players on paper doesn't relate to championships, with the exception of the Yankees and now the Heat in basketball. A couple years ago the Phillies had one of the best starting pitching staffs in baseball (with 3 Aces) and won a championship, but free agency, injuries and players having bad years kept them from repeating. Now they are struggling to play .500 ball and those pitchers are struggling or hurt as is some of their key hitters. Sadly for them those players have large long term contracts and they are stuck with them.

I know that there has to be some arrogance from the players as they need to believe in the team and that they are a key member of said team. Owners and management should not have that same attitude. It's the reason I do not like the Dallas Cowboys, as their owner and GM him basically doesn't seem to get it. I wonder sometimes why he doesn't see the flaws in his team and players the way most of the analysis of the game point out.

I understand you can't cave in to the media, fans and analysis whenever they aren't happy, but if they are all wrong and you are right how come we don't see the results on the field as in your team being in the playoffs. How about winning your conference or having a team consistently having a winning record. Results in sports tend to be wins and losses and you need to have more wins to be considered successful. In some cases enough wins to get in playoffs and then being able to get job done and win championship when you get there.

On that note I will get off the subject by noting the Nationals have joined the Cowboys on my teams to dislike because of their arrogant thinking. I can happily report those Nationals did not make the playoffs this year. The Boston in me can also celebrate as neither did the Yankees.

No sooner do I try to change subjects when another athlete disgraces himself. I wrote earlier about an athlete defending himself against PED's because his sample was mishandled thus could not be used thus he was innocent. The player was a former MVP in baseball and stood in front of the sports world declaring his innocence. This guy went on a holier than now tirade about knowing his body and he would never taint it with these substances.

He is now serving a 65 game suspension for violating the substance abuse policy of baseball for involvement of PED's. This guy was so adamant about his innocence a good friend of his who happens to be the star QB for Green Bay said he would bet a year's salary his friend was innocent. Hope he was lucky enough that no one took him up on the bet.

Right now more people are upset with his betrayal than what he actually did. He's suspended for the rest of this season, but his team is already 19 games out of first place with virtually no chance to make the playoffs. He loses over 3 million dollars in salary for those games, but begins next season with a new contract for over 100 million over I'm not sure how many years. By taking the suspension now he actually saves money and doesn't have to address the media til next year at spring training.

He is the best player for the Milwaukee Brewers, but has admitted to being both a liar and cheater with this suspension and plea bargain he made with baseball. Again the betrayal to teammates, friends, the organization and all those who believed in him is what the sports people are talking about.

How can anyone ever trust anything this guy's says in the future? He made a statement about being sorry, not being perfect and making mistakes so please forgive him. He will start next season and try to regain the peoples trust, but it will not be mine. Like so many he had the chance to come clean the first time but choose to lie and mislead instead.

The Brewers have made him the face of their franchise with that big contract. It will be interesting how they handle it. He's a young star so I'm sure they will find some way to forgive and move on. As I wrote earlier sports doesn't always reflect the "real world of business". He will also become the face of the PED scandal.

If the sports reporters are correct then the Yankees A-Rod is next on deck for this scandal. The big difference is he admitted to using in the past and is an aging star with 100 million left on his contract. Rumor has it the team is looking for a way out of that contract. From my stand point both players are in the same boat now except one eventually came clean the first time the other held onto a lie.

A-Rod is appealing his 211 game suspensions. During his new conference he didn't say he didn't do it, just that he wanted to go through the appeal process. A former player had this to say about all these players getting questioned about their PED use or lack thereof. There are basically two answers, "no" I didn't use them and hopefully are not lying and any other answer which means you may have something to hide. Simple, but as he put it you didn't use them and have nothing to hide or????.

The two teams have similar situations with their players. The difference one team will let the whole thing slide because of the player's ability and the other will try to cut ties because of the player's declining ability. Either way baseballs steroid and PED scandals continue to happen. Did I mention that some of these substances are illegal as well? That makes for some interesting wording by the lawyers as to why and what the players are accepting their suspensions and penalties for.

Here is a crude way to look at it. Some players are using illegal drugs to enhance their performance on the field. What would happen in the real business world if an employee was found using illegal drugs to enhance their performance? I rest my case.

As a side note many of today's players are speaking out against this player and any in general that are continuing to violate the leagues steroid and PED policy. The outrage is such that even the Players Association is having a hard time defending the players who are getting caught.

Is it possible that the majority of players at least in baseball are finally starting to get it? We the fans don't like cheaters no matter who their name is or how bad their judgments were when they used these substances. Banned substances are banned end of discussion. Hello reality break here, no means no and banned means can't use period. The "I'm sorry and just human thing" should not be acceptable any longer, it happened too many times and to way too many players.

Again I'm sorry, but no more excuses if you're caught "juicing" in this day and age then you are blatantly trying to beat the system and gain an unfair advantage over your fellow players. When I was a kid playing sports we called that "CHEATING" and we didn't let those kids play with us. Harsh as that may have been or sound we did not like to play with cheaters or have our team associated with one.

Happily the 2013 football season is upon us and I love both college and pro. Let me start by clearing the air with my opinion about the behavior of last year's Heisman Trophy winner. It was the first time a freshman had won the award ever and that is saying something in itself when you look back at all the great players. This summer the same player is in trouble with a possible NCAA infraction for getting paid to sign autographs. He plays for Texas A&M which brags about an "Honor Code" for all their students.

I went to their website and here is what their code says "An Aggie does not lie, cheat or steal or tolerate those who do". I don't know if he took money or not for those autographs, but

I've heard about alleged arrest for underage drinking and having a "fake" identification. Maybe I'm being a little picky here but the latter sounds like violations of the "lie/cheat" part of the code to me. Not admitting guilt for the autographs the school is suspending him for the 1st "HALF" of their opening game against a much weaker schools football program and the NCAA agrees this is enough.

This kid has put A&M's football program squarely on the map and I'm guessing generated MILLIONS OF $$$$'s revenue for the school and college football in general. Again my opinion, but it sure sounds to me like he violated their Code of Conduct for the University and it is just being ignored or quietly swept under the rug. When did a fake ID and underage drinking become acceptable behavior to any schools CODE?

Sadly I'm afraid the answer is like so many other sports injustices' and it's all about the BENJAMINS, money talks and B.S. walks, what a joke. On the bright side I don't really care about this story other than stating its hypocrisy, because its football season and I have Phil Steel's 2013 College Football Preview which many consider a must magazine to read. I'm using it to make some preseason bets on college football. This is what it's all about.

I have made my prop bets for both college and pro. For the record I'm expecting both Ole Miss and the U (Miami of Florida) to both have better seasons than last year. I cashed my first official bet on opening night when Ole Miss covered the spread by ½ point with a minute to go in the game over Vanderbilt. That ½ point can be a killer as any other bettors can attest.

As for the pros I expect Arizona to have a better season. I also will be playing the NFC to win the Superbowl. I don't care which team it is, the conference is loaded with talent in every division. Just no Cowboys please. Also I expect the Steelers to struggle and not win 9 games.

As for the money issue in college football, more and more players are starting to come out and say they got money from outside people for their performance on the field. Sorry NCAA but your bubble is about to burst wide open.

On the sad side of the story it is the current players who will suffer all the repercussions. I guess it's easy to man up when you don't have to suffer the consequences'. This is truly the injustice of NCAA sanctions. I understand there should be a penalty, but the wrong people suffer the result. Isn't it easy to admit an infraction or crime when you are exempt from the punishment? Way to man up you million dollar babies.

To me there is nothing worse than admitting you cheated when you know there are no repercussions. These professionals that are coming out now about their college violations make me sick. They are like the little kid in school who got away with something and now they are saying NA, NA to the rest of the kids. Yes I'm bitter because they bring a bad mark on all those athletes that did it the right way. I would like to think there are more athletes that did it the right way than those that cheated the system.

Like it or not if you didn't do it the right way you are a cheater. No gray area you knew the rules and violated them anyway, CHEATER. That may not be a popular view and I'm sure many have their reasons, but like it or not you violated the rules. Contrary to belief rules are not made to be broken. Someday these cheaters may actually grasp that concept.

The 2013 baseball playoffs will start next week. It looks to be very competitive. However going into the final weekend of regular season play another Brewer has made the headlines for bad behavior. Apparently the player had been hit by the opposing pitcher in the leg in a previous game and he had wound himself up for payback.

If you didn't see the replay of the incident, then you missed a look that movie directors would kill for on the players face. The Brewer's eyes were so big and white and glaring of rage they were bulging out of his head. That was after he missed the first pitch. The second pitch he crushed out of the park for a homerun. As he trotted around the bases you could see him glaring and yelling at every opposing player he passed.

The opposing catcher came up the 3rd base line blocking him from home plate and if it had been a cartoon the Brewer's head would have exploded he was showing so much rage. The benches emptied and he and a couple players from the other team were thrown out of the game. His face and antics should be the new rallying poster for Anger Management.

As is usually the case he apologized on social meteor after the game. I would call the behavior "going postal", but without the gun. I'm not kidding this guy's face was scary.

Baseball is a sport with some strange unwritten rules or what many call old school. Pitches throw baseballs at hitters to make a point, at times trying to hit them to further make that point. Most of today's pitchers throw in the 90 to 96 mile per hour range, so that ball could be considered a weapon if it happened off the baseball field.

The hit batter is awarded first base. Why not walk him, it gives you the same result and the chance of injury is practically none? Instead of reacting in a violent way don't give him a chance to swing the bat. How frustrated do you thing the hitter would get if a pitcher walked him whenever first base was open. They do it to power hitters like Barry Bond's so he couldn't hit a homerun and beat you. One season he walked over 200 times and often spoke about how frustrating it was not to be able to swing the bat.

Not to sound like a pacifist, but violence isn't always the answer for frustration. Players in many sports let violence overwhelm them during their games and get a minimum penalty for their actions compared to say a court of law. Not to pile on, but not many weeks seem to go by where an athlete at the college or pro level is being arrested for domestic violence.

I know this is a rant, but am I missing something here regarding the idealizing and preferential treatment of athletes?

This just in A-Rod's 211 game suspension appeal is in its first week. His lawyers have filed a lawsuit in his behalf against MLB and Commissioner and they deflected it with having nothing to do with his suspension. Leave it to lawyers to muddy up the waters. This is going to get ugly, but it doesn't matter to me either way. Baseball turned its head on the problem for years so it's not surprising the cleanup is messy.

For the record the baseball playoffs have begun with the Pirates and Rays winning their wild card games to get in. The Dodgers are favorites to win it all even though they don't have home field advantage in National League. The Red Sox are favored in the American League.

More important for me is the NFL is in week number 5 and college football is approaching the midway point. I will watch football over baseball any day, but that's just me. I consider myself a fan of the NFL and sometimes wonder how the General Managers and Coaches evaluate talent for their teams. I also wonder how the heck they keep their jobs when they do it so badly.

I know that I don't get to see everything that goes on behind the scenes with practice and game preparation, but I do get to see the result on the field come game day. So let me quote an ESPN analysis "you play to win the game". I would like to think the Owners run their teams for that same purpose and not the fame that goes along with being an NFL owner.

This may sound naïve or petty, but if your team isn't doing that now and hasn't in the past few years shouldn't they be trying things that have proven to work in the past. The teams with the best records doesn't always win Superbowls, just look at the Giants or last year's Ravens. They do have players with strong work ethics, winning attitudes and Quarterbacks that find a way to win. You don't have to have the best QB, just one that fits those criteria.

Right now there are four teams yet to win a game. Two of those teams have Superbowl winning QB's with offensive lines that are "offensive". The two QB's are struggling big time as well. I understand them staying the course with their QB's. The other two teams are a different story. Both of their QB's have been struggling for over a year. To Tampas' credit they finally made a change at QB along with benching their starter they demoted him to 3rd string and deactivated him for the next game. A bit drastic but it sent a message.

The player answered the message by not going to the game period. It was reported he was asking the team to release him, but continue paying his 6 million dollar plus salary for the year. Being the logical person I am, I felt both actions were wrong on a few levels. I'm told in sports "EGO" gets in the way of reason from time to time on both sides.

My father taught me a valuable lesson regarding employment when I was old enough to enter the work force. It was simple; if you were being paid you did what the employer asked as long as it wasn't breaking the law. If you didn't want to do what they asked, then quit. As long as they paid you for your time you did what they asked. I wasn't a janitor, but I swept a few floors in my day.

Don't worry this had a happy ending. The following week the player was released and the team will continue paying him his salary. "ARE YOU KIDDING ME"! The team reasoned the player was being a distraction to the coach as well as the team and they just needed to move on. If and when the team continues to lose I wonder how many other players will ask for that same consideration. Does the expression "throwing the baby out with the bath water" come into play here? That player just got picked up by another team and they will also pay him 3 million to finish the season. 9 million total, yes I'm shaking my head in disbelief.

Let me continue by noting eight teams currently have only one win, but two of those teams had a bye last week. There are ten teams with 2-2 records and yes some of them have had some questionable at best QB play even with their two wins. That's more than half the league. I will update those stats after this week's games. Here is that update; still 4 winless teams, but two had byes last week, 4 teams with one win and 7 teams are 2-3.

My point is some of these teams need a QB and/or a shakeup. Please don't misunderstand my next question because I'm not a fan of this player, just his results. Why it is no team had brought in Tim Tebow to play QB? Let me do a quick pro/con thing I use for solving problems. I will way the con's against the pros and see if one has a decided edge.

Let me start with what the analysis' and experts say "he can't throw the ball". That is not a good trait for the QB position. The other big con is the media attention he brings with him as he has a big following. Handled correctly I think the media thing could actually be a plus. If your team is as bad as its record says it is they may enjoy the media distraction.

Now the pros, starting with the fact he is a proven winner when he is starting at QB. His Florida Gators won a national title in college. He took a 1-4 Denver Bronco team (that was sinking like an elephant in quicksand) to the divisional championship and a playoff win. His work ethic has been praised everywhere he goes along with his desire to improve. His character is impeccable and he is a very religious man. He has that uncanny "IT" factor about him that no one seems to figure out.

With little or no support from Denver's GM (an ex QB himself) or their coach (whose job he probably saved) he continued to find ways to win. Go back a few paragraphs and you will see a quote about them playing to win games which he does. He can't throw but in that playoff win he threw for over 300 yards and outplayed a previous Suberbowl winning QB. The other team Pittsburgh had a good defense and as I recall were favored to win that game.

Trust me when Denver made that QB change at 1-4 they were very reluctant and said as much. Each week after a win they would give the media all sorts of reasons why they might have to pull him from the next game. To their dismay all he did was help their team win games. Looking at the GM and Coach talk about their wins was comical. You would think they were being forced to eat sore food to find something positive other than the fact that they were winning games.

Tim Tebow didn't even start at QB for the entire season and he has more wins than some of these present QB's have from last year and this year combined. His one playoff win is more than some of these teams have in recent years. By the way that QB for Dallas has only one playoff win and he's been in the league for many years.

Last year Tim was the backup for a bad N.Y. Jets team, I think their record was 6-10 or something like that. The Coach would continually tell the media he didn't feel Tim gave them the best chance to win. Guess what Coach, you weren't winning. To his credit this coach might be one of the best defensive coordinators in the league. On the flip side the owner and GM made him coach, so he's over his head.

I honestly feel it got to the point that they were afraid to make the change. If Tebow started winning games the way he did in Denver the fans would be screaming for both the Coach and GM's jobs. The Coach and GM at Denver had to eat a lot of humble pie.

The brain trust in Denver was so supportive they would offer Peyton Manning the keys to the city to come play for them. I can only wonder what other perks might have come his way during the negotiations. They knew it would take an established icon to appease their fan base and move the winner out of town.

Again I'm not a Tim Tebow fan, but I still think he would be an upgrade at QB for several teams and win more games for even more teams. The man just finds a way to win games. It just might be possible that those losing teams are like the Jets. If they bring him in and the team starts winning games they would have to find a reason to tell their fans why they waited so long.

Not that money matters to these teams, as Tampa just spent over 6 million dollars for their exiled starting QB to stay home, but Tebow actually generates revenue. Two of those 0-4 teams play their home games in Florida where Tebow is a cult hero. Just a wild guess on my part but his fans might actually by tickets to see him play. His jersey sales might match the entire rest of the teams total for the year.

As for that 6 million dollar salary figure per year, it might be an unlucky figure. Seattle paid that out for an unproven free agent QB and he couldn't win the starting job from their 3r round draft choice of that year. They in turn moved him to Oakland which would continue to pay him that same salary the next year.

This time the same QB didn't win out the job and was the backup again. He would get his chance to start in week 4 because of injury. Sorry to report he played terrible and got the same demotion the QB in Tampa got. It will be curious to see if they too cut him and continue paying his salary. They just cut him a week later, but will pay his salary for the year.

Many professional teams throw around lottery type money to players, and then if it doesn't pan out say something about the good of the team, pay the player for the duration of contract and cut them loose. They do the same with coaches'; see L.A. Lakers for that one.

Am I missing something here, seriously? Are you kidding me? Dag nabit Muskie, I would love to have had an employer pay me big bucks not to work for them. That QB that went to both Seattle and then Oakland is investing his money wisely I hope. Seattle hit the jackpot with that 3rd round QB, but Oakland may consider Mr. Tebow for a culture change. You know "WINNING".

Here are three different teams that invested way too much money in busts at QB. Two of those teams could fit the "elephant in quicksand" metaphor I used earlier. Heck what do I know? I'm just a fan who likes football and will occasionally make a wager on a game.

For the record I don't watch Tampa or Oakland games unless they are playing the Patriots. No I don't even watch them when they are the only game on. Add the 0-4 Jacksonville team to that list. Let me know when they get an NFL worthy QB or at least one that wins games.

Somehow I feel better, almost lighter now that I got that off my chest. Jacksonville is now 0-5 and has scored 51 total points.

Games on the line late in the 4th quarter and neither teams defense is stopping the others offense, Peyton Manning against Tony Romo, who you got? To their credit Romo's offense was playing the best game they had ever played and Denver one of the worst defensive games ever. Dallas had the ball with around 3 minutes to go, but had their backs against the goal line. I had just finished telling my dogs how Romo usually throws an interception in these types of games and didn't he do it. He threw into triple coverage, while his running back was open just to his left and underneath all the defenders. Manning ran the clock down and they kicked a field goal with no time left to win the game.

The owner and GM for Dallas would praise his QB and team for playing the best game he had seen them play and call it a moral victory. Dallas is now 2-3 but tied for first in their division, a testament as to how bad the other teams have been playing.

So I will close this chapter with a simple question. Would you rather have an exciting team that is losing and not making the playoffs or one that tends to be dull and wins ugly and goes to the playoffs? If it's the first then the Tony Romo lead Cowboys are definitely your team. If you like seeing your team in the playoffs then get a winning QB, I know it's' not that simple or is it.

Bottom line for these teams with losing records a change is coming, at QB or coach, probably both. Happily no matter what the owners and GM's do the 2013 football season goes on. It's now week 14 and the coach for Houston was just fired with a record of 2-11, with the 11 being a current losing streak. One down and I'm sure more to come. By the way their problem is QB play. The starter was benched mid- season and the backup has yet to win a game.

So here we are mid-December of 2013 and the NBA season is 25% complete and there is a shocking trend developing. The East Conference has two teams with winning records and both are well above average. As for the West they have ten teams with winning records. I don't ever remember such a huge gap between conferences. Yes it's early, but this is pointing to a huge injustice come playoff time.

Sadly I don't care, as I realized last night I haven't watched one game this year nor care too. Yes I have become a victim of the mediocre product that the NBA now puts on the court. It has become a star driven league with few exceptions, the biggest being the Spurs. The super stars/ best players are taking the majority of the money leaving little to build a supporting cast of players to make a solid team.

The NBA has a salary cap as do all sports these days to protect the owners from themselves. They have luxury taxes to penalize the over spenders and give that money to those keeping within the cap to share. Here's the problem, a best player is being paid 25% of the salary cap on his team.

An NBA team will suit up some 12 players plus a couple on injured reserves and the other 75% of the cap money needs to be spread amongst them. If you have two stars then you are paying them close to 50% of your cap money. It doesn't take a math major to see how small the pie becomes for the majority of your team.

When a young team develops through the draft it takes a few years to really get to become playoff caliber. Then the best players leave for the big money or demand it from the current team leaving less for those role players just like the better teams.

Now some of the stars that have already made their money group together with similar stars and take less money so the pool for the role players is a bit higher see the Miami Heat. The gap becomes the young star getting his max contract. They sling the usual bull about it not being about the money just fair market value. Then when they get paid 25% or more of the cap and the team isn't winning they whine about the caliber of the rest of the team.

To date there have been no players who can match 25% of their teams overall play on offense or defense. It's simple math and now the product on the floor is showing the flaw. Sadly the trickle-down effect is showing up in college basketball with the one and done rule. The young stars with potential play one year then go into the pro draft. Teams pay them good money to become pro players instead of them learning in college and getting a nice education at the same time.

So it's time for this fan/viewer to move along to something else, but like those star players who proclaim "it's not about the money" let me leave with a few other reasons. I actually played basketball growing up so I'm familiar with the rules.

That great crossover dribble the analysis love to applaud current players for having as a skill was called "palming" in my day and it resulted in a turnover. As for those running thunderous dunks featured on Sportscenter highlights, many would have been called "traveling", another turnover. Count the steps on some of those great moves under the basket, 2 or more is traveling.

Basketball brought some nice moments in my life both playing and watching, but until they come back to Earth with its management I'll find something else to do with my time. I could read more books or heck maybe even write one.

Before sending the book into the Publisher this just in on the A-Rod case, the Arbitrator has made his ruling and the suspension was reduced from 211 games to just the entire 2014 season including post season. A-Rod still proclaims his innocence with no failed drug test and calls his accusers going on a witch hunt that is out to get him. This story was such a "hot topic" the next day 60 minutes spent more than ½ there show going over some of the evidence and interviewing some of the people involved. By the way A-Rod chose not to appear but his lawyer did and defended his client vehemently.

Using baseball terms let me spin my take of this fiasco. Before I start let me also mention that A-Rod has admitted to lying in the past as has the chief witness against him. So you have one liar proclaiming the other liar to be lying about this particular situation. So here's how I look at the evidence.

Baseball has thousands of "text" messages between these two men over a long period of time. They are on their private cell phone numbers and appear to be coded for their interpretation only. Unless they are best friends, which they proclaim not to be why so much communication? Called strike one against A-rod.

Next there was a $49.5K money transfer from one of A-Rod's accounts to the other parties' lawyers whom they sent back and he claims was some kind of clerical mistake. We are talking some serious account numbers being shared to make this type of transfer. If nothing is going on how do you get those account numbers or even know who his legal team happens to be? Called strike two.

Lastly if you're so innocent why not testify in your own behalf, instead deflecting your position as the same as the Commissioner of Baseball, who chose not to testify. Sorry but that's called strike three and per your own games' rules three strikes and you're out.

Yes it's a lot more complicated than I just broke it down to be and A-Rod will appeal to a real court of law, even though the arbitration decision was supposed to be final. He claims to be paving the way for other players with his actions.

The decision we the public have is which liar is actually telling the truth this time. That's the problem with being a liar, when you do tell the truth how can people belief you? Bottom line baseball now has their poster boy to hang the steroid era on. Smile A-Rod and step aside Jose Canseco. What a sad abuse of talent.

Also what a long chapter, I hope those not liking sports hung in there.

4

POLITICS/POLITICIANS, CAN'T THEY JUST GET ALONG

I'm writing this chapter during the fall of 2012. President Obama will be opposed by the past Governor of Massachusetts (my home state), Mitt Romney. For the record I am a registered Independent voter. I like to feel free to vote for the best person for the office they are trying to attain.

Personally, I would like to see the two main political parties working together to help solve the problems of our country. Yes I'm a dreamer, but things really need to get better. I honestly believe that if one party had the cure for cancer the other party would oppose it for any number of reasons. Both parties preach things need to get better, but not if it's the other parties idea. It's really quite sad when you think about.

Growing up politics was never discussed by my parents. It was a topic my father felt was up to the individual person and both sides could be fanatic with the arguments about the issues. It wasn't allowed in our home and if we were visiting someone and the conversation changed to politics my father would leave the room. If it continued he would actually have us leave. He felt his views were his own and did not need to be argued or explained. He was definitely old school.

The negative ads and miss information that goes out in the political ads is what really bothers me the most. Depending on your political view memories can be rather short about issues and how we got there. It's amazing how a candidate can be so pro for an idea earlier in their political career or during a previously held office then do a complete 180 on the same issue. It happens a lot when their party line is different from their original view and now they are trying for a higher office and need more party support.

I'm about to share some of my views and opinions, remembering they are mine and I don't expect everyone or any one to agree. By the time this book is published the Presidential election will be over so these views will be a moot point. On the bright side for me I get to vent and get them off my chest.

First thing we need to remember is where the country was during the last Presidential election. The economy was so bad that President Bush had to bring in both candidates that were running to replace him and brief them on the situation. He was opening the lines of communication hoping for some ideas. I actually thought that was the best thing he ever did as President, but that's my opinion.

My financial portfolio was going downhill fast as was the entire economy. Both banks and major automobile makers were on the verge of going bankrupt. The bottom was falling out of the housing market for multiple reasons. They were complicated issues and there were no easy solutions. As I recall unemployment was in double digits nation wide, which further complicated the mess. I would be remiss if I didn't mention we were ending our 8th year of President Bush a Republican as President.

The country needed a change of direction and a lot of economic help to turn things around. As the new Presidency began the Dow was going down and the talk was going from recession to depression. Personally my portfolio was down over 25%. The Dow had gone from over 10,000 points to around 6600.

It was obvious to me that the problems that got us here were over time and would take time to get us back on track. As we know one of the partial solutions were for the government to bail out the banks and automobile companies that needed it. It was not a popular solution at the time.

Here we are four years later and the automobile industry seems to be back on their feet. The Dow is up over 13,000 points. I'm happy to say my financial portfolio has come completely back and has actually made close to a 25% gain. Again I'm no financial expert but that seems like a pretty strong come back to me.

For those of you whose portfolios didn't come back the way mine did, don't blame the President, and instead look at your financial advisor. If you listen to the opposing party they would tell you things aren't much better than they were or should be better depending on the ads. All I can say is how it affected me and where I am today. My portfolio went from at least a 25% deficit to a 25% gain. If my math is correct that's a 50% improvement from the bottom.

Another ad that comes to mind is that unemployment is at 8% under President Obama's watch and that it unacceptable. I agree that 8% is not a great number and needs to get better. The fact being overlooked is that it was over 10% nation wide before it bottomed out from the old regime. That's a 20% improvement in 4 years and we seem to be coming along on the right track. Hey don't kill the messenger the facts are out there. The Republican Party is trying to make these improvements seem bad, when in reality they aren't.

Could the economy and unemployment get better, absolutely? That doesn't change the facts that both have been turned around and are improving. Another hot topic has been the Presidents try to improve healthcare for the nation and make it mandatory, you know it as Obama Care.

I honestly don't know if it's the right answer, but it's time we did something about it. Other countries have plans that work copy one I don't care just get something that works. Here's the kicker for me as a resident of Massachusetts, we have mandated healthcare. It is compliments of Governor Romney, the same man running for President. Only now he doesn't feel it's right for the whole country because that's his Party line. Come on really, it's the right thing to do for the State but not the Union. Using that logic maybe he's not the right President for Massachusetts. If elected, do we get to throw out our mandated system, or just not acknowledge him as President?

I'm hoping that you're seeing some of my points even if you don't agree with them. The bottom line is like it or not President Obama has made improvements. Whether you feel they are coming fast enough is another story. That being said remember he has to work with the Republicans to make things happen and they haven't exactly been speeding up the process or cooperating with him.

Here's the dilemma I had during the 2004 Presidential election, I wasn't happy with the current President Bush who had gotten us into a questionable war overseas after 9-11. He was going to clean up terrorism and make Bin Laden pay for what he did. He was going after those weapons of mass destruction. To that he found no weapons and no Bin Laden. By the way President Obama took care of Bin Laden; you are welcome Mr. Bush as it was one of your "main priorities".

Unfortunately his opposition was a Senator from Massachusetts by the name of John Kerry. For the first time in a Presidential election I did not feel either candidate was capable of running our country. President Bush had already proved it to me during his four years. Mr. Kerry just didn't seem to have the passion or positive assertion to handle the job.

As we know President Bush was reelected and the rest is history so to speak. During those next four years, no weapons of mass destruction and no Bin Laden, not to mention the economy went into the tank at the end of his term. Again we were trending down in 2004 and reelected the President anyway. Now we seem to be trending back up. The choice is up to the voters.

I will leave this hot topic with something my father-in-law told me about a conversation he had with a town councilman. This man told him that most people don't know what's really good for them, but the political officials do. It was just one mans opinion but it makes me skeptical of all politicians because of it. It does aggravate me when I vote for a candidate because he is pro something, then they get in office and changes their position on the matter.

Just sharing some thoughts and ideas and will go to the next subject with this final thought. Vote wisely, the person you elect to office represents you, but it's his ideas he will be trying to implement.

As with the sports chapter some of the things I wrote earlier have actually happened. President Obama was reelected and is still fighting with the Republicans. The Dow is now around 14,500 and my portfolio is improving right along with it.

It's the beginning of October of 2013 and we have just started a government shutdown. Yes our fine political leaders could not agree on the budget. Actually that is not quite the case in this situation. One of the political parties is trying to appeal a health care bill along with their budget concessions.

Again it's not that simple, but Obama care was passed by the people. The opposing party has tried unsuccessfully to repeal it some 40 times, I'm told. I did not research that 40 number, but it is the number talk shows are referring to. The people have spoken through the electoral process and want this health care system. They reaffirmed their support by reelecting the President who supported it and was going to implement it.

I'm not a huge political person and I don't know the inner workings of our political system. Like it or not the people want to give this health care system a chance. I don't know if it's the answer, but you need to start somewhere. I can't say I've heard the other party come up with a better idea other than status quo.

Let me point out the President was for tighter gun control as was the majority of people. It was voted down by Congress even though the people seemed to be for tighter measures. I don't see the President attaching repeal to this decision on other bills the way the other party is fighting this health care bill. The bill went into effect the same day as the government shutdown.

People are outraged with the government shutdown and its costing millions of dollars a day. The opposing party will make a few concessions to open parts of the government back up, but not the health care issue. People are losing wages and some businesses are being affected as well. Don't worry those political leaders that caused this shutdown and lose of taxpayer dollars are still getting paid no lost wagers.

Since I have a tendency to be a bit sarcastic let's add a few other addendums for Bills some politicians would like to repeal. Prohibition, a woman's right to vote, right to bear arms, and here's one for those die hard southerners slavery. Heck we only had a civil war over that one. Go down south and spend some time in non-tourist areas and you will find many of them are still bitter they lost. Some feel they won, but didn't get the result they wanted.

Hopefully you see the sarcasm, if not seek some help. I recall something about government for the people, not the party's political agenda. Somewhere along the line some of our political leaders have lost sight of the "for the people" part of their job. The DOW has dropped 500 points since this shutdown started. Do you think it's affecting the economy or just a coincidence?

5

TELEVISION ANOTHER POPULAR WAY TO PASS THE TIME

I watch way too much TV, my wife and kids are always pointing this out to me. In my defense I suffer from chronic lower back pain which I take medication for several times a day. Trust me when I say I have no pain free days. My recliner has a massage and heat setting which does give me some comfort (recliner broke during move and my replacement doesn't have heat and massage). I'm not going to bore you with the rest of my health problems, but they cost me my last job, which is why I have time to watch TV and of course write this book. I do a lot of walking around the house as well.

Back to the subject at hand, other than sports there are a crazy amount of police shows on TV. Apparently the producers of these shows don't mind flooding the air waves with them. I must admit I do watch most of them even if it's on reruns. I'm sure I will miss some but let me try to give you a night by night breakdown of them.

Sunday you have Glades based on a detective in southern Florida. It is followed by Longmire which is about an old school sheriff who doesn't even own a cell phone. Really an officer of the law without a cell phone, in this day and age? It's based on a community bordering an Indian reservation and some of the conflicts that develop along with the crimes being committed. That takes up 9-11 that night if there isn't a better sports event to watch. Sorry but Sunday night football will beat that out. That's why they have On Demand, what I great feature that has become.

On to Monday, where you have the remake of Hawaii Five O with a new kick butt leader to show them the way. Unlike the old version it has a sub plot following why the lead character's parents were killed. The show is up against Castle who happens to be a mystery writer following a female police detective solving murders. I'm sure this happens in many large city police departments, we just don't hear about them. Yea right, I know it's only TV, they do add a potential love interest between the two lead characters.

Tuesday is the back to back NCIS followed by NCIS in LA. Both about detective teams solving military murders and thwarting possible terrorist acts. One east coast the other west coast and occasionally they help each other. It's usually followed by some type of CSI program from a different city. Up against the Los Angeles version you have Rissoli & Isles based out of Boston. Here you have a homicide detective working with the medical examiner to solve murders.

These CSI shows are everywhere and change days and times depending on opposing programming. One's located in Vegas, another Miami and let's not forget about New York. Somewhere in there is Criminal Minds, which can appear any day or time as well. This show features FBI profilers for all types of murders.

I know I said I would give you a day by day breakdown but I'm only through Tuesday and the list is getting long and they are always changing days to fill slots. Thus let me just throw out a bunch more that haven't come up yet. Person of

Interest is about a super computer giving a name of someone who needs help but doesn't tell them why or where they are, the maker of the computer and his ex-special forces associate need to figure why the name came out. Throw in Unforgettable, about a female policewoman who has a photographic memory and can play back any thing she sees back in her mind, in case she missed something. This was an interesting show but may not be coming back.

Let's not forget Rookie Blue, which I feel insults rookie police officers and I will leave it at that. Blue Bloods is about a family with all the adult members in some form of law enforcement fighting crime and or the system. It does make for some interesting plots. Can't forget all those Law and Order shows with the special victims or units or any other version they can come up with. Their reruns are everywhere.

If I've missed some I'm sorry I probably never watched them or they didn't make an impression. You must admit I have mentioned quite a few. Only sports have more shows than crime drama's. Speaking of sports how many channels do we need to dissect the same game. Look at ESPN, with ESPN2, ESPNU, ESPN Classic and ESPN NEWS and CBS is starting to get into the act not to mention Fox. During the college football season you can see different games on all their channels, but the news reporting is basically the same info on all those channels.

Then there are all those Fox sports channels to cover every area in the country. They specialize in the sports teams of their own districts especially college teams. Once again they show their own sports teams during the different seasons.

Depending on your Cable company or if your get Direct TV or the DISH you get even more sports offerings. Let's not forget the All Season passes for as many games in a sport from around the country. NFL, NBA, MLB, NHL, College Football, NASCAR and even Soccer now have there own channels. If you can afford it and like all those sports it could literally become all you watch during the different seasons. Let's not forget that each major sport also has its own channels that air year round 24-7.

Again depending on your cable offering there is Horseracing from around the country. Unlike the other sports channels they offer you potential online web sites to bet those Horserace's as well. I wonder if the other sports will be far behind. I should point out that not all states allow it, but with anything there are ways to get around it I'm sure.

You can even access the Web on your TV now. Not to mention program recordings of shows you would like to watch later. You can even watch TV on your computers and on airplanes. Basically there are very few places where you can go where a TV isn't present or nearby.

The cell phone has become as popular as TV and is literally everywhere. You can't go anywhere these days without someone's cell phone going off. I will save this rant for another time. The cell phone has become the Swiss pocket knife of this generation. Yes you can watch TV on it with some "App".

For the record the only thing I can do with my cell phone is answer it and make a call out. My wife programs my needed numbers and gets any messengers for me. My phone is rarely on, except when I am away from my wife. No exaggeration I don't think five people have the number and mostly because it came on their caller ID. I don't make many calls so I don't get many. It's a great system. Thus I have more time to watch TV, again back to the topic at hand.

I mentioned the "On Demand" feature we now have access too through our various providers of TV services. In some cases it cuts the commercials' way down as in a 60 minute show becomes 45 yes its magic. Other times you can Fast Forward by them.

Let's not forget TiVo as well. So basically if a show or movie aired through your provider recently you can watch it. Right now my wife and I have about 5 shows on TiVo. That being said we literally watched 17 episodes of a show we hadn't been watching from On Demand in just a few days. O My G. They thought sliced bread was big in its time, look where we are now, progress?

To date myself a little more the first TV my father bought was "Black And White". I'm talking caveman days, my first pet was a dinosaur, just ask my daughters'. Your sports experience were the local pro teams and Wide World of Sports, even my mother watched that. There was the occasional major league game during the week. If you were lucky, a couple college football games on Saturday followed by the same for Pros on Sunday with the local team catching the spot light. Yes these were dark times, literally.

I did not watch much TV as a teenager and no video games at the time either (still don't play video games). My friends and I actually went out to play, you know outdoors. When I was home I actually would read books, how primitive. Today that type of behavior would be considered radical possibly in need of therapy. OK I exaggerate again, welcome to my families' world.

So basically I eat, sleep, watch TV and take care of my personal hygiene. It's not really that bad I also handicap horseracing (which I wrote a book about). Might as well give it a plug "Tips For Playing The Horses". Guess what it's about? I share my handicapping on Facebook no gimmicks. Buy the book, read the dedication and you know the page. What a shameless plug. As this book will attest I'm also continuing with that writing thing.

I made that above statement to compare my life with that of a dog of which we have 3, but they don't watch TV. Now that I write this not sure it was the greatest idea, but hey your still reading. Once again I bring up my father-in-law as he would point out how great a dog had it and would gladly come back as one. Eat, sleep and do its duty outside. The sad part is I was going to point out how much better my life is than a dog.

Pathetic that TV is a big part of that. Now that I'm depressed on to the next subject, maybe the wife and kids are right I need to get a life or help, probably both.

6

ABUSES AT WHAT POINT DO
YOU MISS CROSSING THE LINE?

I know this is a weird subject, but lately on the news this seems to be happening all over. You read newspapers and see news reports on TV almost daily of some form of abuse. I'm not just talking about what we do to ourselves with rape, child molestation, physical assaults and the list goes on. How about the environment we have to live in and the animals and other living things that share it with us?

What triggered me writing this chapter now was the series of incidents that happened with the Rutgers basketball program and how it was handled? Most of the facts are somewhat hearsay but let me share how I saw it unfold.

Apparently in late November/December a tape became available showing how the coach was physically and verbally abusing his players during practice. My drill instructors in boot camp weren't that outrageous in their actions. That was my initial reaction. The Athletic Director and apparently some members of the Board of Trustees viewed the tape and made the following determination. Suspend coach for 3 games fine him $50K and sent him to some type of anger management sessions as it was deemed a first offense.

The problem was the tape covered several practices possibly over 3 years and they treated it like a first offense. It was multiple practices how could it be a first offense? The AD defended the action and felt he had done the right thing and apparently the other witnesses of the tape agreed. The President of the University had left it in their hands and supposedly did not watch the tape at that time, maybe the word ABUSE wasn't used in describing it to him I don't know.

As the story unfolded it was revealed a man hired for Player Development had notified the AD about the behavior during that previous summer. His contract was not renewed and was let go. That did not match the story of the AD. The story broke on ESPN and at that time the President decided it was time he looked at the tape, better late than never. You definitely don't want this guy as a first responder.

According to his interview a couple days later he felt the coach needed to be fired immediately as did most of the media coverage which were outraged and that happened. He also felt the AD needed to go and he resigned the next day. He tried to explain how he delegated the initial decision to his AD and a few Trustees, which in hindsight was a bad idea he admitted. The AD got over $1.2 million plus other benefits when he left to avoid any legal hassles. That's what I call a nice package to walk away from the job. It's also came out that one trustee felt the coach should have been fired but was over ruled. By the way the school lawyer has now resigned.

Personally I think those Trustees and maybe even that President need to go as well, as they clearly failed those young men on the basketball team. Those poor young men were at the mercy of that coach's abuse and any retaliation or complaining could have cost them in regard to the team. I will also note that the Assistant coach resigned the next day as well. Three jobs lost maybe more to come for what was definitely some bad judgment by the men in charge. Even more disturbing is how highly educated these people were supposed to be as well. The Trustee who agreed with punishment is now under scrutiny as well.

Let me continue with a little background as to how I was brought up so you have an insight as to how I may look at things. My father worked heavy construction from the time he was 16 and my mother was a stay at home mom. We were considered middle class and it was the 50's and 60's. We attended a Protestant church and my father helped out on Sundays. He had a title but I can't remember what it was at this time.

Both my parents were involved in Cub scouts. My mother a Den mother and my father as Scout leader, my dad also followed me into Boy scouts as a leader as well. My dad also coached the young boys for the church basketball team for many years. They were the youngest group and my dad made sure everyone played at least one quarter no matter what the score or even in the playoffs. He was well respected with everyone associated with any of those organizations and especially the parents.

When I was bad my punishment was to go to my room and think about what I had done. If you watch NCIS you know Gibbs likes to slap his subordinates in the back of the head when they made mistakes, my mother would do that to me on occasion as well. My dad was about 6 feet 2 and weighed around 220 lbs so no force was necessary to get his point across.

It was very disturbing to me when I witnessed or learned that some of my friend's father's would actually hit them on the bare backside with a leather belt. Some of those friends were girls which was more disturbing. In Junior High I learned that the Nuns at Catholic schools would hit the students across the knuckles with wooden rulers as discipline. Not sure which offense was worse, but today those actions would definitely be considered "abuse".

My parents may have been pioneers as they taught me never to abuse a younger child, girls/women or animals. It was just wrong unless in self-defense. It's just what my father would consider "common sense" which seems to have gone the way of the DODO and Dinosaurs.

Not many weeks go by where some form of child abuse physical or sexual isn't reported. Almost always by someone in a trusted position that has the authority of those under them just like the story at Rutgers. We're talking about highly educated people here and/or positions of authority. The fact that religious leaders abuse this privilege is even worse to me as they are people of the cloth so to speak.

Some will say it's caused by an illness, accident or just their own abuse when they were a child, but ignoring it is not the answer. Moving the abuser to another location isn't the answer either. I hate to say this but in some cases we just might need to clean up the Gene pool. Sure I'll get some hate mail for that one. Inmates in prison don't tolerate prisoners that come in as child molesters and look at how exconvicts are treated in our society. Much worse than these highly educated college Presidents or Trustees that let these things happen on their watch.

Once again I'm sorry but admitting you might have made a mistake in this type of situation is inexcusable. To continue paying the offender after the fact or letting them continue the same job is crazy. In the real business world this type of behavior is usually dealt with immediate termination in most cases. I don't think they give you any nice going away gifts as well. When you have a video tape of the incidents in question and still are debating it makes me question the leadership ability of all involved.

I'm not big on religion but what happened to "Do unto others as you would have done to you" or something like that. Let's treat their sons or daughters like that and see how they feel about it then. I would like to think their concern might be a bit higher when it's closer to home. It's easy to turn the other cheek when it's not your cheek.

At what point of time does blatant child abuse or any abuse for that matter need to be addressed? After injury or death, or in this case a damming video? Sometimes, gee I'm sorry or I made a mistake doesn't cut it, just ask the inmates. I know there is much worse abuse happening in the world than this incident, but maybe it's time to draw that proverbial line in the sand and say enough is enough.

As my dad would say, "enough, stop beating the dead horse". After all it's the highly educated here that aren't recognizing the problem or its severity. On to the next subject and hopefully a more pleasant one for those still reading, let's get the blood pressure down a bit.

Sadly I wrote this chapter during the winter of 2013. So this next chapter will be about another type of violence.

7

TERRORISM AND
MURDER/SUICIDE

Today was the Boston marathon 4-15-13 and it will definitely be one for the record books and not in a good way. Several hours after the leaders finished the race and the bulk of the crowd was assembled a couple of small bombs went off at the finish line. As of this writing at least two people are dead with multiple injuries. When it first happened a news station had some raw as in uncut footage that showed people right where the first blast happened.

It was like a scene from a horror movie, lots of blood and a man walking towards the camera with an arm missing. They immediately changed to another view when they realized what they were actually showing. I just don't get this kind of action under any circumstances or duress. To me it is plain cowardice to blow up innocent people for any cause.

A few months ago a young man entered an Elementary school with an assault rifle and started killing innocent children and their teachers. What is wrong with people? Just how messed up or disturbed are you that you feel killing helpless people is the thing to do under any circumstances. Neither group of people deserved what happened to them.

Let's not forget the 9-11 incidents that really woke this country up to terrorism. More innocent people used as a tool to make a point or statement about something they had nothing to do with. The saddest part of all is the people behind these acts truly believe they have the moral high ground with these acts. When did killing innocent people become the right thing to do when proving a point or protesting something you feel is unfair?

Don't insult my intelligence by comparing it to the causalities' of war either. I know we have many cultural differences throughout the world, but this type of behavior is just plain wrong. They should change the word terrorist with cowardice. Instead of giving these types of people any form of what they seem to be looking for they should just refer to these as another act of cowardice. Let's be honest it doesn't take much of a man or person to plant a bomb and walk away or shoot people who are unharmed and helpless.

As for those suicide bombers who seem to think they are doing a noble act and sacrificing their life while doing it you're wrong. If you seriously think that is the right thing to do then just commit suicide, because you are seriously "you know what". Come on if you think killing yourself along with or after killing innocent people is the proper thing to do you have issues.

That's where the murder/suicide doesn't make sense to me either. I get the fact that you're unhappy, I suffer from depression myself I know how low a person can start feeling. Just because you're unhappy or disappointed in someone else or yourself doesn't give you the right to take their life because you've decided to take your own.

These types of acts are so wrong in so many ways I find myself shaking my head in disbelief. Have our morals and teachings gotten so bad that we are actually tolerating this type of behavior in some way? Somewhere along the line the concept of respecting our fellow man has gone by the way side. As my father would say "our society seems to be going to hell in a hand basket".

If nothing else would you want somebody or group of people to do those things to your family, love ones or friends? If your answer to that question is anything but no you need help. Not to be harsh but sometimes you are the problem not the people around you. If it has happened to your family, that is truly a terrible thing that has happened to you. Taking other innocent lives is not the answer.

It's these types of people that make me think the death penalty might be the proper solution in some cases. Once again I can see the hate mail coming, but I don't want these people ever getting back out into society. I see no reason wasting any money on them to keep them alive under the circumstances either. The person doing the murder/suicide condemns themselves to death should a terrorist who causes peoples death not suffer the same fate?

There's another old saying about not being able or willing to do the time then don't do the crime. If death is the penalty for taking someone else's life maybe some of these people will think twice before committing the deed. If that thinking is naïve on my part or radical sorry, but at least we will be cleaning up the gene pool a bit (yea more hate mail).

I'm just tired of innocent people being killed for no reason. The school shootings that have been occurring bring me to gun control. The guns may kill the people, but it's the person that pulls the trigger who is to blame.

That being said do we really need assault rifles in our home? Last time I checked we weren't at war in our own country or on the verge of invasion. Just my opinion, but assault weapons for Joe average American seems to be a little over the top.

I like to think of myself as a somewhat reasonable person, are my thoughts and or ideas that far off base? If so then so be it this is America and I'm entitled to my own opinion or so I'm told.

It's the next day after the two bombings with 3 dead and over 170 injured. Of the 3 dead one was an 8 year old boy who was there with his family to greet their dad when he crossed the finish line. Reports say his mother was injured and his sister had to have a limb amputated. Add 17 to the critical list, many of which will need multiple surgeries to help repair their injuries.

Again in what world is doing this kind of harm to so many innocent people remotely justified? All those people were there celebrating both the day (Patriot's) and the event of the marathon. It's an international event, just check the countries from which the winners came from. I know it's not the first time an athletic event was targeted, the Olympics' come to mind.

You truly can't understand the anguish this type of tragedy has on people unless it happens close to home. This is an event that I actually attended when I was younger. I have friends that go to this event every year like people do Times Square for New Year's Eve. Happily I have not heard of any of those friends being injured, but the fact remains they were there.

Once again this is cowardice in its truest form. Every time something like this happens anywhere in the world I have the same thoughts and feelings about how senseless these acts are in the scheme of life. I'm not a religious man, but my thoughts and my form of prayers go out to all the people affected by this atrocity. I'll come back and fill in some updates like other chapters as they warrant, but I need to go to a happier subject.

So here is that update, two suspects were identified and their pictures broadcast across the TV networks. They were located and there was a shootout killing the older coward and injuring the other who was able to get away temporarily. An officer was killed and several injured during the sequence of events.

They were brothers here from another country and apparently unhappy. The younger coward was seen in the Watertown area and authorities locked down the area and began a massive search. He was located hiding in a boat that was perched behind someone's home and not in the water. Another shootout and he was captured and taken to hospital where he was in critical condition.

Today he was charged in his hospital bed with "using a weapon of mass destruction". This comes with the possibility of the Death Penalty. The authorities feel the two acted alone.

Again my applause to all the law enforcement groups that worked together to identify and capture these two cowards. The tragic event happened Monday afternoon and Friday night one was dead and the other in critical condition. That is people and organizations working together to bring the whole situation to a quick end.

There are many questions to be answered, but those two troubled young men will no longer be part of the problem. Those first responders, medical personnel at the scene and all those law officers will be honored and remembered for a long time to come.

BOSTON STRONG!

8

FOOD IS ANYTHING TRULY GOOD FOR YOU OR UNTAINTED?

I 'll go out on a limb and say we all eat even though our tastes and habits may vary very drastically. As the years go by many of us will find likings for foods we wouldn't touch as children. Be honest I'm sure there are many of you out there who hated vegetables, but enjoy them now.

Another factor that goes into our food choices can be attributed to the person preparing them for us when we were younger. Mom I loved you, but you may have been one of the worst cooks whose food I've eaten in my life time. It may have been the reason I actually thought the food in boot camp was pretty good.

People joke about some meats being overcooked and tasting like shoe leather, well my mother's pork chops could have been a cobblers' delight. There's an old word "cobbler" referring to a person who works on and repairs shoes. Back when I grew up when the soles of the shoes were wearing out or possibly developing a hole they were brought to the cobbler. We had one a block from our home. My father used to say we kept him in business putting new soles on many of my shoes. Hey I was a boy and tough on clothes in general.

Back to the pork chops, they gave new meaning to the phrase chew your food. No kidding supper was the only meal you were allowed to have a beverage with at my home. I can't say I ever heard my father complain about the cooking, but on weekends when he was home he did the cooking. He was actually the one that suggested I have water with my chops as he probably noticed the hard time I was having swallowing them. Once I had a glass he quickly followed.

My favorite meat is beef in the form of steaks and prime rib. I discovered my liking for this food after being discharged from the service and was no longer subjected to military or my mother's cooking. I was eating meat you could actually penetrate with a fork and cut with a knife, not hack like a saw. Trust me when I say we were a meat and potatoes family with very few variations.

Yes I mention potatoes because my mothers' could be flattened out and within a couple minutes become a dried up solid object. Once again sorry mom but you're cooking sucked.

My wife is 100% of Italian decent whose grandparents came over from Italy. She can flat out cook and her mother was even better. When we married I weighted less than 130 lbs. I ate food I had never even heard of while we were dating. Holidays' especially Christmas was an extravaganza of food. Their relatives could cook as well and we would visit several of them on Christmas and Christmas Eve.

Christmas Eve with them is seafood night and plenty of appetizers and desserts to please the palate. These women can mix up some desserts you would dream about later. Although I haven't had the opportunity to eat many, her cousin Carol makes the best cannoli I have ever eaten. One of my better friends married her, lucky guy.

Going to Cynthia's different Aunt's homes and getting to sample their cooking was just as delightful over Christmas holiday. Just a side note I got my appreciation of wine and scotch from her father. There were plenty of both flowing during the 2 day event of Christmas and the Eve before. My wife did the driving as she was not and is still not a drinker. I probably make up for both of us which might be TMI (my daughters tell me that means Too Much Information).

Her family would get a nice laugh at my expense as not only hadn't I eaten many of the foods they ate regularly, but I hadn't even heard of many of them. Remember the meat and potatoes thing at my home, I was not kidding my exposure to food was very limited. Although we did go out for pizza once in a while my food experiences were very non memorable growing up. My wife actually makes pizza from scratch, my oldest daughter will request it sometimes when she's' stopping by for dinner. My wife's mother would make pizza almost every Sunday night, making a visit something to look forward too.

Needless to say it wasn't long until I crept up to 140 lbs. and a whole pants size. We're talking real porker here, just kidding. I know that weight can be a very touchy subject with many people not just women either. I would laugh when my male friends would inform me they were on a diet. Did I have a lite beer? Are you kidding I didn't and still don't drink lite beer and very rarely had it in the house unless someone else brought it.

Hello I'm rambling, back to the subject of food. I ranted about TV earlier in the book and food has its own shows as well. My cable company started with the Food Network, added the Cooking Channel with some of the same chefs from the other channel.

Rachael Ray a chef from Food Network got a morning show on prime time, a one hour slot to show some cooking, along with having some interesting guests just like the other morning talk shows. I will admit we have several of her books, including places to go eat in different states. Actually we have gone to some of them as well. Went to one in Nashville and asked if the chef would autograph my copy of the book at their page. To my surprise they didn't even know they were in the book.

The wife has attempted several of those 30 minute meals, but with prep work they always take over an hour. They are still worth making as some of those recipes are delicious. Sandra Lee is another of our favorites and we have several of her books as well. Yes we do use them. Something about those cocktails to serve with some of those meals really steps it up for me.

The new show to the party is the afternoon show called "The Chew". I will just say it is one of the shows we have on our save recordings program (DVR). We bought the book and cook some of the recipes from both the book and the show. We do not put the amount of HOT ingredients that they sometimes use, but we haven't had a bad meal yet.

Please remember my culinary exposure was nonexistent growing up. Today is Wednesday which was "Prince Spaghetti day" at my house, just like that old time commercial. It was a highlight for meals to eat at home, as my mother could open a jar of sauce and boil water with the best of them. Sorry again Ma, but none of my friends ever wanted to stay for dinner.

I know I seem to be throwing poor mom under the bus over the cooking, but she only served two types of pasta. Spaghetti of course on Wednesdays and sometimes for lunch a dish I still make for myself today. My wife and daughters find it disgusting and will not even try it. Its elbow macaroni boiled, drained al-Dante, and then reheated with tomato juice and a can of Vienna sausages cut up and added to it. As my wife likes to call it "elbows and tomato juice", she always forgets to mention the sausages or whatever mystery meat is in those cans.

I'm not kidding these were the two meals she made the best. However on weekends my dad would whip up some tasty concoctions. He would make a variety of different tasting muffins along with pancakes and French toast. On Sunday he would make a roast beef on occasion and it was medium rare. We would eat that beef in sandwiches for the rest of the week depending on how long it lasted.

To show how much I appreciated my wife's cooking my weight actually crept up to 170 lbs. over the next 15 years. Then one summer I perfected a recipe for banana daiquiris' with vanilla ice cream, banana rum and of course banana's. Our next door neighbors Tom and Cathy spent a few evenings and weekend afternoons sharing a blender or two of these delicious drinks. I gained 30 more lbs. to crack the big 200 mark.

It was that same summer when I trained for an "all-you-can-eat" lobster/steak restaurant buffet in Rhode Island. The training was easy, when I felt I was full from supper I would just eat a little more to stretch my stomach out. Thinking back on it what the hell was I thinking? Anyway one Saturday evening those same daiquiri neighbors took us to the buffet.

I honestly don't remember what it cost, but there was a two hour time limit for you to be there. You would have thought the four of us hadn't eaten in days the way we attacked that buffet. The steaks were cooked to order and I had three. As they were being prepared I devoured 10 lobsters with minimal vegetables. The women went after the jumbo shrimp with gusto and saved room for desert.

Showing some decorum I did not eat dessert, but the three of them ate a Key Lime pie by themselves and then some. To wash everything down the women showed some "suave in the cabase" (just a phrase and word I made up years ago) and drank water while Tom and I had two 16 oz. gin and tonics. They didn't ask us to leave right at the two hour marker as they saw we were getting ready to pay the bill and waddle out. The four of us were miserable walking to the car. We laughed and joked about everything we just ate as we drove away. It was still early at night so we went to a nightclub and attempted to dance off some of the food we had eaten. We still talk about that night to this day with fond memories.

As you can see a big appetite I had, but far from healthy. I never had a weight problem and could eat most foods with no regrets. Cynthia had been on diets before so she would try to make as many healthy type meals for the family as we would let her get away with. I would discover the best diet secret and change of eating habits that can ever happen to anyone.

I can assure you that I now have my eating habits under control. It came in the way of diabetes. Talk about a diet change, I lost 28 lbs. the first month. It brought me back to the 170's and there I stay. I'll refrain from discussing diabetes at this time, but will give you a few food changers I had to make.

I had a coke classic to drink with my lunch every day at work no matter what I was eating. After dinner I would have some type of snack usually chips or popcorn and wash it down with a 32 oz. Powerade. I no longer drink either and have substituted water for both. Water has become my main beverage of choice as I do not like any type of diet soda.

I'm proud to say that I have been able to control my blood sugar with my diet and do not need insulin. When diagnosed it was 399 and now it stays around 120. Unfortunately I now need to watch what I eat and or how much of it I do eat.

I mentioned beef being my favorite food, when younger I would eat it as often as I could. Then came high cholesterol and my consumption of my favorite food had to come way down. In my defense the first time I was ever tested for cholesterol was a couple days after returning from a trip to Las Vegas.

During my visit I was having steak and eggs for breakfast. Hitting an all you can eat buffet for lunch and they all served sliced roast beef along with all the trimmings. Trust me when I say I was eating my money's worth at these buffets. Top the night off with a steak or prime rib. My cholesterol never had a chance that week. No my wife was not with me so I was eating what I wanted when I wanted and as often as I wanted.

I really enjoyed eating and I had a metabolism that was burning it off for those early years. Now with the diabetes, high cholesterol, high blood pressure, acid reflux and a word I can't spell or pronounce so I will call it the inability to digest nuts and seeds, well my food choices and amounts I'm allowed to consume have become very limited.

I endeavor to persevere, which means I grumble a lot about my current food choices as compared to what they were. Not many days go by when my wife or daughters' don't ask "should you be eating that?" They already know the answer so I tell them I need the Zinc. The comic Elaine Bosler (sorry about the spelling) used to refer to her consumption of M&M's in that way. It sounded good but had no substance or truth for that matter.

The wife and kids tend to shake their heads at me a lot and not just over my food choices, but I will save that for another chapter. The point about food for me is to enjoy it. There are a few things I know I can't have and I avoid them, soda and nuts mostly. Others I have in moderation or my version of moderation.

My wife and I still love to go out to dinner with friends or by ourselves. We just try to make more healthy choices and go out less often. When in Vegas I only eat beef once a day, OK twice tops.

I have my wife's family to thank for my increase in the variety of foods I eat. At restaurants I don't always order the steak or prime rib, I actually try other dishes. Duck has become one of my favorites and I will order it most times when available. I know and enjoy many different Italian dishes not just spaghetti. Occasionally I go off the reservation so to speak and order something I've never eaten before.

Those rare moments get some quizzical looks from the wife along with some snide comment. Variety is the spice of life just not much spice for me thank you as I'm quickly approaching the 60. My digestive system just isn't what it used to be.

One of the things I've learned about food is to enjoy your favorite items to eat when you get the opportunity to do so. Another is if you don't try new foods then you will never know if you like them or not. I remember the good old days when my oldest daughter wouldn't try anything new especially seafood. Then she did her mother a favor and tried some lobster, opening the flood doors for what she likes to eat now.

Again I was lucky when it came to discovering food and all its varieties including how it gets cooked. As I wrote earlier my wife is a great cook. We will watch these cooking shows and if something catches our attention she will check into making it. Several chicken dishes have been added to our dinner cycle. We do eat our share of chicken but the wife really knows how to mix up its preparation for consumption.

For those of you who have fallen into a rut regarding your eat at home meals it doesn't take much to break out. If you have no cook books then print a simple recipe from one of the cooking shows websites and give it go. It's easy for me to say that as my wife does all the cooking. Fortunately she enjoys it and likes to eat just like me, only smaller portions.

For those who don't cook like myself or aren't good cooks I feel your pain. Like I said earlier I got lucky with my marital choice regarding food and many other things as my wife would point out. Before meeting my wife I ate a lot of fast food with few meals at home. When the opportunities came up I accepted all dinner invitations that came my way. Might have even thrown out a few hints here and there if I thought there could be a good meal in it.

Life is short eat what you like and enjoy it, you only go around once. The chapter name may not have fit what I just finished writing, however think about what you eat. Did you grow it, catch it or have any input as to how it landed on your plate? Even if you choose to eat healthy or a certain way, did the growers or people preparing your food keep everything natural? If so how? With acid rain and chemical fertilizers is anything really pure and natural anymore, just food for thought?

9

DEPRESSION EFFECTS MORE OF US THAN YOU KNOW.

I suffer from this condition/disease and sympathize with those of you who also live with this condition. It can be debilitating and literally suck the life right out of you. I'm sure that I was showing symptoms for years before I actually was diagnosed. My family and I have a saying for when one of us is ignoring a problem hoping it will go away (they never do). It's called swimming in a river in Egypt "Denial". I know it's a bad joke but I find myself there more often than I care to admit.

Many of you that have depression or have someone close to you who does will relate to some of the things I'm about to point out regarding depression. For those of you still wading in the "Denial" stages hopefully this will help you look for some help. For years I had convinced myself that I was coming down with the flu or a cold and would spend a day or two in bed hoping to stop it from getting real bad. The "it" was the draining feeling that had overwhelmed my mind and body. Then I wouldn't get either and think I did the right thing. As it turned out I was just ignoring a bigger problem.

My wife tried to tell me for years before I actually went to talk to someone about it. Like many I was sure this was not the case and my body and possibly mind was just getting run down and needed a break. Alas these run down days came more often and I finally did something about it. For those who can relate here's a series of events in my life that triggered a serious period of depression. If you relate or know someone who does please seek the proper help or try to get them to seek it. Sometimes you just need a hand.

Change is not my friend and the bigger ones can be paralyzing. Let me go through that recent series of events that triggered some tough times for me. Cynthia and I took a trip to New Orleans to meet a long life time friend Karen and spend a few days enjoying the city. It was the spring of 2013. Having severe lower back issues flying is not something I do often and the two flights on Sunday to get there took their toll. I ended up spending Monday in our hotel room while the ladies toured the city. I was in a lot of pain and not happy that I had to waste a day recuperating.

The rest of the visit went OK and we took our two flights back Friday. I spent most of Saturday and Sunday laying down hoping my back spasms would let up. As much as I enjoyed being in New Orleans I can tell you the pain of flying put serious doubts as to my doing it again. The thought of not being able to travel once in a while for vacation was very depressing. Unfortunately that was the start of series of events that would continue my downward spiral.

A month earlier I had to change health insurance carriers and made sure to pick one my primary care Dr. was affiliated with. I had been with this man for almost 30 years and there was a huge comfort level. This man was the best Dr. I had ever been associated with as he would actually follow up with you about lab work the next morning. I'm talking old school care and commitment.

The trade off in keeping him was losing my Pain Management DR. who I had been with for almost 10 years. He was one of the best as well and told me he would let my primary care DR. know which prescriptions he wanted me to stay on. A year or two earlier my diabetes DR. had left the area and my primary care Dr. had taken over my care and monitoring of my blood sugars and prescriptions, again huge comfort level there.

For a multiple of reasons, none of which were my business, my Dr. had transferred his practice to a local group. He had assured me that he would be giving me the same care and this group offered some other services that would help make the change a smooth one.

Anyway that following Monday after coming back from New Orleans I needed a refill of my pain medication (morphine) that my pain Dr. had been prescribing. I called the Dr.'s office and that's when the bottom was about to fall out of my world. The receptionist answered the phone and I told her I was a patient and whom my Dr. was, before I could continue she stopped me and told me my Dr. had suddenly retired the previous week while I was in New Orleans. Letters were in the mail. It felt like my life had just come to a screeching halt.

As I sat there in disbelief she continued by informing me I would need to see a new Dr. before getting any prescriptions refilled. Still speechless on my end, she told me there was an appointment for that Wednesday would I be able to make it? Of course I would make it as I needed the refill. Fortunately I had enough to make it a couple days. Yes panic was starting to set in and the walls seemed to be getting closer.

My memory has gone the way of the Dodo so I can't remember all the thoughts that were going through my head when I got off the phone. I can tell you none of them were pleasant. It took a few minutes to regroup and then I let the wife know we had both lost our primary care physician of many years. Let the downward spiral continue.

One thing I've found out about depression is that negative thoughts can overwhelm positive thoughts very quickly. All of a sudden everything is becoming negative and you feel your spirit just leaving your body. I had no control over that series of events and was feeling about as helpless as I had in a long time. That free fall of negativity would continue as I would learn later I was now going into a world of red tape.

The next couple days are a bit fuzzy as my thoughts were strictly with the new situation with my health care. I can't stress enough how I felt the rug had been pulled out from under me. Wednesday arrived and I showed up for my appointment a ½ hour early.

As luck would have it my old Dr.'s receptionist had come to the new office with him and she was kind enough to come out and talk to me. I must have had that deer in the head lights look as she tried to assure me I was in good hands. Have I mentioned that I'm somewhat of a skeptic when it comes to change?

After a few minutes the nurse calls me in and checks my vitals. Shockingly my blood pressure is a bit high and she asks if I'm having a stressful day. I quickly go through the bomb that was dropped on me and yes I'm a bit stressed. That was before I met the new Dr.

To say my new Dr.'s personality was totally different from the old is a huge understatement. To his credit he was very professional and came across cold as ice. To sum it up their association had protocols involving the medications I was prescribed and he was not comfortable prescribing them. He would give me a two week supply and have his office set me up an appointment with another pain management clinic that took my new insurance and they would prescribe the pain meds

I had been taking for years. Or as it turns out make what they considered necessary changes. There's that "change" word again.

Just in case there was a problem getting an appointment with the new clinic he would see me again in two weeks. I checked out, got my appointment for two weeks and was told they would get back to me within 48 hours with an appointment for the clinic. For those of you with depression you know uncertainty is not our friend. The clock was ticking on that 48 hour period as I left the office.

A week later I got the call to set up the appointment with the pain clinic. My wife had suggested I call after the 3rd day, but I was swimming in Egypt. Let me also point out that life was moving along during this whole process. By that I mean the regular activities you do during your normal life. I was dragging myself through those days waiting for that call. I wasn't just lingering in "denial", I was floundering in it.

We had moved a few months earlier and had downsized into an older home. We knew that a few things would need to be addressed to fix up the home but were hoping they might be put off a year or two. Wow were we wrong, as the oil burner was the original and the home was over 50 years old.

The hot water lasted for less than a minute. Did I mention we moved in during the month of December and lived in Massachusetts? The new burner was put in the day after Christmas, cha ching. During those two weeks waiting for that burner showers were few and far between for me. Our 3 dachshunds didn't seem to mind and the wife did a lot of head shaking (I get that a lot).

During those two weeks we also determined that the kitchen we were using wasn't just small it was dysfunctional like our family. Let me tell you remodeling a kitchen aren't cheap, but it had to be done. That project had been completed and paid for just before leaving for New Orleans. Between those two projects and all the little things we had fixed add another $20k or more to the actual closing price. This doesn't cover the new roof we need in the spring or air conditioning, which will run around $12K tops. Hope I'm not dreaming about that cost, as it turned out I was as it came closer to $15K.

Somewhere along that time frame our youngest daughter and her husband informed us they were having a baby. This would be their first child together as they both had one from previous relationships. My youngest daughter C.J. has a daughter named Lily who is 5 going on 20. She has my wife wrapped around her finger. Her husband Dan has a son Alex who is 7 and a hand full. They are having a boy much to the dismay of Lily and my wife.

Needless to say life was moving along at a brisk pace for me. For those of you who do not suffer from depression you would consider many of those events I just described as part of your normal life. Life throws you a lot of curveballs that need to be dealt with on a daily/weekly/monthly fashion depending on the issue. Trust me I understand you need to figure things out as you go.

All the above being true doesn't change the fact when depression starts to set in it's tough to stop the downward cycle. It can be like a train that you can't get out of the way of as it comes down the tracks. This is why a frequently asked question I get from my healthcare people is "Do I ever think about suicide"? Sadly I must admit the answer is yes. During that two week period waiting for the new pain clinic appointment you could up that to "hell yes".

They don't like that answer and it always leads to a few more questions on the subject. The other day while at the new Pain Management clinic that was one of the questions, the "yes" answer prompted this immediate question "has it been in the past few weeks"? I had explained the health care changes and DR. Retirement earlier to her, but not everything I just wrote about. After all we had just met and I couldn't even remember her name (there's that memory thing again, it's sadly missed).

With little hesitation I answered yes again. Again those of you not struggling with depression might find this response shocking and alarming, as did this nurse. Her concerned look told me she was not happy with that answer and offered whatever help she could give me. When I assured her things were fine now the questions stopped. Truthfully I had considered a way during my drive to that appointment, but I figured it would pass like . the rest.

From there I was passed on to another nurse who took my vitals. Yes my blood pressure was a bit high again. I see a pattern forming there. Then I waited what I considered a long time before actually seeing the DR. They told me it might take 2 hours for the entire appointment. It was close to 3 when I left so you figure out how long I waited. I had fallen asleep in the exam room and when I came out to the desk to see how much longer, the looks on their faces told me that they had forgotten about me, such a reassuring feeling.

After all that no medication even for what I was currently on. It was their practice no medication on first visit. However they did set me up with a follow up visit the next week. The run around from the new wave DR.'s was now complete. I understand the pain meds my Dr.'s have been prescribing me are considered heavy duty, but they were necessary and I always followed the dosages as prescribed. There was no abuse on my part and always got my refills when they were scheduled, never early.

Even with these meds I have no pain free days. I will purposely limit my activities when possible so I can skip the pain meds on some days. The depression attacks both your mind and body. Having my lower back issues only complicates things for me.

This whole health care issue is far from solved; hopefully it will be before the depression wins the battle. Besides getting my pain issues all straightened out my short term goal is to finish this book. If you're reading this book then I'm still winning the battle.

For those of you struggling along with your depression I wish you well. It's easier said than done, but take one day at a time. Try to solve your everyday problems one at a time as well. Find thoughts that keep those negative ideas at bay and relish those good moments when they happen. Another thing that helps is remembering those good people in your life and what they mean to you and vice versa.

Another fact I should point out about myself is that I am the "king" of procrastination according to my wife. It's probably true as I do like to really think things over before doing them. Take this book, it's been in my thoughts for years and I'm just writing it now. I'm not impulsive and tend to be on the lazy side. I write this so that you know just because I think about things doesn't mean I would actually do them.

How many people think about what they would do if they hit the lottery? Or maybe daydream about other things that will probably never happen. I'm just saying we don't always act on our thoughts. That being said if I had the opportunity to help people at the expense of my own life I don't think I would walk the other way. The odds of that happening are probably greater than hitting the lottery. I do live a rather boring life.

I have talked to a couple different Dr.'s and counselors about my depression and would recommend others to try this form of help. Strange as this may sound, sometimes it helps to just get it all out. According to my wife that is another flaw I have, bottling things up like a pressure cooker until it's ready to pop. I characterize that as not being spontaneous.

Yea, yea, I know I need help and not just for the depression as my family is quick to point out "I'm a piece of work". That's a good thing right? The bottom line for me with dealing with the depression is to try and limit those bad days. When having them I try to do things to take my mind off the problems that are getting me down.

Life really is a precious thing and should be enjoyed whenever possible. Funny how things happen at the strangest times in our lives, yesterday I spent most of the day in bed. It was my back pain that put me in bed and my depression that kept me there for the day.

Even though I have been writing this chapter about depression I could not stop the helpless feeling my back pain was giving me. As I've stated I try to limit my physical activity, but still try to do a few things, just in moderation. Our new home needed some serious landscaping both front and back. We hired a landscaper to fix and maintain the front and Cynthia and I would work on the back.

Please keep the laughter to a minimum as moderation for me is no more than an hour's work at a time, usually less. Since yard work is one of the most brutal things on my back I decided to limit my activities to 45 minutes or less. This way I thought I could go out 2 to 3 times during the same day and chip away at the backyard.

Cynthia could last longer and did, but she kept reminding me not to overdo it. I honestly thought I was managing my time well and found that after 30 minutes it was time to stop. Through the course of the day I went out 3 times and was quite sore by end of day. Knowing the soreness would linger throughout the night I took a nice long hot shower and instead of a pain killer took a muscle relaxant. I was hoping it would help me sleep.

I went to bed early feeling good about how nice the back yard was starting to look and how well I had paced myself. Sadly that feeling didn't last long as the pain continued to get worse and I found myself getting up almost every hour. I was awake when the sun rose and miserable from the back pain. The door was open and the depression was walking in again.

On the bright side recognizing what had happened I was able to think through it and here I am on the second day writing about it. Yes my back is still very sore, but I didn't let my depression keep me down for long. Sadly this is a rare triumph for me as usually the depression lingers. I think writing this chapter at this time helped get me over the hump.

For me this is one of the small victories against my fight with depression. However those small victories are what keep me going. When we finish the back yard it will become an even bigger victory, especially if I don't have to spend any more days in bed to recover.

So here I was ready to go to the next chapter, but before I do I had to go see my new primary care Dr. this morning. My blood pressure was up and it happened to be up the last two times I was at his office. It was also high when I went to see the back therapist. This encompassed 4 appointments in less than a month. My blood pressure medication could be increased as my present dosage was fairly low.

So we agreed to double the dosage, read into that what you will I surely did. It was also noted that my body temperature was 97.6 and has been under the average of 98.6 for those same appointments. He already had a letter from the back Dr. and knew about the proposed change in my meds in that department as well.

He answered all my questions and I felt we were starting to connect the way I had with my old Dr. I mention both facts as while these things were happening I could feel the depression building within me. I actually felt and still do that he had helped me get through a tough morning that was spiraling downward for me.

Again my sympathies for those who truly understand this feeling, everyone else I hope you never do. Even though I know the signs sometimes I need some external positive to help stop the avalanche of negativity.

I like to play the horses, actually wrote that book I mentioned earlier. This coming weekend is the Oaks/Derby at Churchill which I love to handicap and watch all day for both days. First race is at 10:30 Friday morning, but I see another back specialist at 9:30 the same morning. It's a 45 minute ride. I'll miss a race or two, but I'm hoping for a good day anyway.

We will be discussing and possibly change my medication for my back. There was mention of some kind of patch that uses some type of slow release. Also more pain point injections (one of which is like a spinal for those women who had them during child birth you understand the pain). My new primary care Dr. explained the entire report to me as I mentioned earlier. The man knows his business.

Those little ups and downs to most people can become mountains and sink holes to those of us with depression. I consider myself a fairly intelligent man, the fact that I know and recognize the signs and still get sucked into these depressions just adds to my negativity.

Bottom line with the back the new pain Dr. and I agree the patch could be a positive change. When my morphine runs out in 30 days we will start with the patches, hope there's no withdrawal. Oh by the way they require a mandatory drug abuse seminar. No seminar no meds or change of meds. So that will be coming up within the next week.

To be honest I was curious as to what they talked about nowadays regarding drugs. Over 40 years ago it was pot smoking leading to heroin shooting. Even at the time I thought that was a huge leap. Anyway here I was going through more change and procedures. For the normal person this could be another day in the life, but not for me.

The light at the end of the tunnel so to speak was that I was seeing my depression DR. within the week. Today that light was attached to the train that was coming down my tracks. His association did not take my new health insurance and this was my first scheduled visit since I had changed. He would discuss any refills I might need but to see him it would be $125.00 for the visit.

I left and drove around the corner to my new association to see who they recommended. To my amazement within a few minutes the receptionist sent me downstairs to people who help depression and gave me a name for someone to talk too within their organization. This was one of the new services my old DR had talked about regarding this new Association.

I got off the elevator feeling good only to find the room she sent me to was Radiation. Hey everyone is trying to save space these days so I figured they had condensed offices. To my delight the new receptionist confirmed my assumption. Yes this was the right office and there was a person that handled depression. She would look up the number and I could be on my way and call back for an appointment. My cell phone was in the car so I immediately decided I would call from the parking lot.

I never got that far. I know what the hell could possibly happen barring a natural disaster? She couldn't find a business card for the depression department or one for the person who was there "right now". After going through the phone list for the building no number there either, "hello", you just told me the person was around the corner as in down the hall. So she gave me two phone numbers for their two offices further away from where I lived and suggested I call them and see if they could get me in touch with the office I was standing in.

Hey you can't make this stuff up. I walked out and went to my car in a state of disbelief. I sat in my car hooked the seatbelt, started the car and then looked at my cell phone shook my head and drove off. I let the windows down and just started home. My wife was at an appointment and I didn't want to interrupt her with a phone call so I would wait until I got home.

I was starting to free fall. I mentioned my blood pressure had been up over the recent weeks, but I didn't mention the increase in migraines I was having and how much longer they were lingering. I felt like I was having chest pains, but was sure it was just the stress that had been building up. I'm writing about it now so I guess it wasn't life threatening.

I'll be 60 next week and was thinking that might be a fitting day to die. Yes this thought went through my head and still is as I'm writing this. At this very moment the negatives are far out weighing the positives. So here I am trying to think about all those positives to change my train of thought.

Here's the one that sticks out in my mind, our 34th anniversary is two weeks away. She deserves better than me, but the facts still remain she loves me and I love her. That's worth sticking around for. So to keep the positive energy flowing I'm going to do something I really enjoy, handicap a few horse races.

One of the things that have kept me going through the rough times of my depression is the thought process I just shared with you. The thoughts would be different for other people but the process might still help. Here I am the next day feeling a little better about things. After washing up and making some coffee I went right back to the handicapping that I enjoy.

For me that was a way of keeping some positive energy flowing. It's the old adage doing what works for me. Hope my sharing can help others get through similar bad times. It sounds corny but you need to believe there are better times ahead and you just need to get to them.

For the record Cynthia took me to a nice restaurant the night of my birthday. The food was great and so was her company. We had some laughs and my spirits were uplifted. Lobsters went on sale the week of our anniversary so we picked up 6 and had a nice dinner at home to celebrate the day. Unlike those lobsters I steamed, I remain alive and kicking.

Sadly the change with my blood pressure medication has not been helping the way the Dr. had hoped. I have been feeling terrible and almost passed out at the grocery store, so back to the DR. I went today. We reviewed all my current meds and the other Doctors who had prescribed them.

He now understood that I had lost all my old Doctors and he was my life line so to speak. Happily he could connect me with a Cardiologist right in that facility. His office would also help find someone to help with the depression. No med changes until I see that Cardiologist.

The Cardiologist set me up with a stress test which I failed. She felt I had blockages and needed to have a specialist do a small procedure to check my arteries. It was called Angioplasty. So after some blood work the procedure was scheduled for the next Monday.

The specialist called and gave me the breakdown regarding what he would be doing the next day. It sounded simple but it did involve him looking into my heart and going through an artery to do so.

I fought the negative feelings the days leading up to the procedure so that I could have a positive state of mind. As it turned out no serious blockages just 30 to 40 %, so the only change was from a regular aspirin each day to a children's. Take it easy for a few days which I am very good at and everything should be fine.

Happily everything healed fine and I just got a huge black and blue in the area they were working at. The follow up visit with my Cardiologist a week later reiterated what the specialist had found.

This could have been a very depressing situation for me, but happily I was able to calmly get through it. The specialist did tell my wife I was a bit anxious and rambled a bit during the procedure. Oh yes I forgot to mention you are awake during the procedure which I attest to my being a bit anxious so to speak. Considering he was going into my heart while I was awake I thought I handled it rather well.

10

FAMILY FOR BETTER OR WORSE

I'm 60 today and had a terrible night's sleep. I couldn't stop myself from going down memory lane as I lay in bed. This is not the happy chapter I was hoping to dive into after that last one, but it is what's fresh in my mind.

My family was not close knit. My oldest sister is 14 years older than myself. When I was 3 she joined the Marines, when she got out she married another Marine and they lived on the West Coast, California. I honestly never had any memories of her from those first 3 years. My parents rarely talked about her and we never went to see her family while I was growing up. I would learn later that she was considered a wild child. Her teenage years were the 50's and she might have been the female version of James Dean. Her name is Dixie Lee which had something to do with music I think.

Not sure how it happened but I have her High School picture that she signed To Mom & Dad Love Always Dixie Lee. She had to be around 17 years old at the time and I must say she was a very attractive young woman. You should see the hairdo from that time.

My other sister was 7 years older than me and yes the big joke for our relatives was that my father had the 7 year itch. I also have her High School picture with no writing on it. Her hair is a bit longer as she was a product of the early 60's. Not to sound prejudice here, but she was an attractive woman as well, her name was Melody Jane. Until now I never noticed the two pictures have some similarities.

Both have their arms crossed with the top hand displaying their High School rings and both have religious crosses around their necks. One is wearing a short sleeved sweater and the other long sleeved and they are facing opposite directions. They do not look like sisters and I'm not sure we were that religious growing up. We went to church but that was it.

Before airing the family laundry so to speak let me try and recall the extended family as I remember them. I had no living Grandfathers growing up. My Dad's mother died when I was around 5 or 6. My mother's a couple years after that.

They both lived in Maine as that's where my parents were born and raised, yes "maniacs". Sadly I remember nothing about my Dad's mother. As for my mother's, twice a year she would stop for a few days on her way to and from Florida. She lived with and traveled with an Aunt and I don't know what side of the family she was on, guessing Ma's.

My mother had a brother living close to my Grandmother in Maine as in next door. Also a sister and brother living close together in the Haverhill, Mass area. The brother in Maine was nicknamed "Gib", don't know why, but his wife was "Snicky" again don't know why. I figured out his real name was Maynard as his son was Jr. As for my Aunt I don't remember her name, sorry Aunt Snicky.

My uncle was retired military with a pension. I vaguely remember us picking him up at a military base and driving him home to Maine when he retired. He was one of those people who really enjoyed life and loved to laugh. He and my father could tell funny stories and jokes for hours. It's a shame I never remembered any of them.

Aunt Snicky was a nurse and enjoyed life as much as my uncle did. Looking back at her she would be considered a "fox", not sure how she ended up with my uncle. They had one child whom I already mentioned. A cousin I haven't seen in years.

My mother's sister Ruth (lived in Mass) died of cancer when I was in my early teens. She was married to a man named Joe with two boys Jr. and Johnny. Those boys got into a lot of trouble and I will leave it at that. Not sure what my uncle Joe did, but he seemed to get a lot of deals and bargains for things falling off trucks. Again my memory isn't great and I will leave it at that. It's been over 40 years since I've seen them as well.

Her youngest brother was "Bub" which I think was a nickname for Bob. His wife Betty was the spitting image of Olive Oil, maybe skinnier. They had the big family of four I think, two boys and two girls.

My father had a brother "Hadley", don't know if that was his actual name and two sisters Pat and Elaine I think. Pat lived on the west coast and Elaine in Maine. Again it's been a long time. They all had children, but were older than myself so I didn't really know them.

Except for my grandmother's trips to Florida none of them ever visited us that I recall. My dad would drive us up to Maine over the 4th of July and sometimes Labor Day weekends for visits and that was about it. I would spend an occasional week in Maine during the summer.

I was young and ignorant as to what went on with the extended family. A product of my upbringing I didn't know much about a family dynamic.

The 50's and 60's were a different time to say the least. Watch some of those old movies and you will get a feel for how things were back then. Almost all adults smoked or at least those my parents associated with. They enjoyed their alcohol as well. Dean Martin was big back then and he had a show on TV. He openly smoked and drank on the show. My mother thought the guy was great and we had all his records they were 33's back then.

People basically could smoke almost anywhere they went except church. I may have had friends whose parents didn't smoke but I can't remember them. Everyone smoked in public unlike today where that type of behavior is against the law. The "No Smoking" areas were just starting to appear. They were located right next to the smokers which made no sense to me.

Anyway Dean would smoke, appear to drink hard liquor and tell jokes and sing on his variety show. My mother loved this guy and unfortunately emulated him somewhat in real life. I would learn later that she became an alcoholic some time during my high school years. She was a chain smoker as well, 3 packs a day was the norm. My dad would tell me later that she would smoke in the shower, no I never figured out how.

Hey ignorance was bliss for me back then. I never thought twice about my mother napping during the afternoon when I returned from school. Again I don't want to sound like I'm bashing my mother, I loved her but she had problems. Her smoking and drinking got so bad the Dr. was nagging her to slow down and maybe consider stopping.

She did stop, that is, seeing the Dr. Sadly she kept the Dr. thing from my father, as he would discover the truth too late. My mother weighed less than 100 lbs soaking wet but she was a tough old broad. She could drink with the best of them as well.

Back then Friday was pay day and my mother couldn't wait for my dad to get home. It was a quick supper then off to the package store. The routine was 3 cartons of cigarettes, a case of

16 Oz. Duke Premium beer (this was true donkey piss) and ½ gallon of blended whiskey.

My dad had caught me smoking around the age of 16 and made a deal with me, he would stop if I would. Yes we both did, thank you dad it was one of the best things you ever did for me. I mention this so you understand the cigarettes were all for my mother. If she ran out before Friday night she was out of luck. Needless to say she could be very touchy on those Friday's when she ran out.

As for the alcohol my dad liked to have a beer each day when he got home from work and of course my mother would join him. Depending on his day after dinner he may have another and occasionally a highball. My mother would always join him. I would learn later my father did not want her having any alcohol until he was home and having one himself. He would discover that she was sneaking some during the day. My mother's drinking and smoking was the only things they ever argued about. By Friday both beer and whiskey were gone.

My dad was a stickler for the routine at the package store. Even if they ran out of beer or whiskey he would not buy anymore until that Friday night. My poor mother had some tough Thursday nights and Friday days and even I knew why.

To me what my parents did was normal I just assumed everyone else's did the same. It wasn't until I was in the Navy that my sister Melody sat me down and explained things to me. Sadly it was after my mother was diagnosed with cancer. Since she had stopped going to the Dr. by the time my dad found out it was completely through her body.

The Dr.'s couldn't believe how she could stand the pain for so long without seeking help. She actually fell and dislocated her hip the day before they were leaving to drive down to Florida. No one knew how she could handle the pain, but she refused to see a Dr. and they drove to Florida.

The day they arrived, my mother couldn't handle the pain any longer and allowed my father to take her to the hospital. It was all downhill from there. She knew something was wrong for a long time but had no intention of changing her lifestyle.

I will not go into the surgeries she went through over the next few days; finally the Dr.'s told my dad there was nothing else they could do. She refused to stay in the hospital so somehow my dad drove her back home to Mass. She was sedated the whole trip.

At the time I had no concept of what my poor father was going through. He had to watch as his wife of close to 40 years withered away and died before his very eyes. There was no Hospice back then so my sister Dixie flew in from California. With the help of Melody the two of them took care of my mother during the day while my father worked.

During this time I applied for a hardship discharge and came home every weekend. It was a brutal time in all our lives. I would learn later that my father had informed all the relatives of my mother's condition. He let them know if they wanted to see her before she died they needed to come quickly.

Not one family member from either side of the family ever came to see her. I will spare you the details, but she died a few weeks later on a Friday night. The funeral was Sunday and no one from my father's side attended. The relatives that did come literally drove down, attended the service and went home.

I don't know if my dad had a few words with them about how disappointed he was that none of them came to see her before she died. To my knowledge he never contacted them again or them him. I didn't and have not contacted any of them since.

My father never spoke to his brother or sisters again. I got the discharge and returned home to help my father through the next few months. During this time he contacted and old friend who had lost her husband. She could relate and helped him through that tough time. He did not want to be alone and asked me if it was alright if he married her.

I understood his need for companionship and let him know it was fine with me. I wanted him to be happy. Apparently that didn't sit well with my mother's side of the family either which may have attributed to why they never tried contacting us again either. After a few years my father retired and moved to Florida with my step mother. As I said our family had a strange dynamic.

Before he left he sat me down and tried to explain the whole family thing to me. He had saved the address book with all the phone numbers and addresses and wanted to pass it on to me or my sister. I told him Melody or Dixie could have it or throw it away I was in the process of living my own life. I don't know what happened to it and really didn't care at the time sadly I still don't.

It was the 70's with Sex, Drugs and Rock-N-Roll for me. Looking back there could have been a little more sex as I rarely had a girlfriend. Any way my sister Melody stayed in the area and we always stayed in touch. She had married and older man by some 15 to 20 years, but you could tell he loved her.

They would watch me grow my hair long and enter a wild phase which I may write about later. The names will definitely be changed to protect the guilty in that chapter.

My sister Dixie already had her family, a boy and girl with an adopted girl. I had met my nephew and niece one summer when my sister brought them to our home for a few weeks. She was having marital problems and needed a break and some time to think. Her husband did some job with on the road sales thing and I'm not sure he was being faithful. It was none of my business and again I was young and naïve at the time.

Melody had just started her family and named her son after my dad and I, yes George Robbins Atwood. Not long after a daughter Elizabeth. I would visit here and there and called her once in a while, they lived about 45 minutes away. Again I was trying to live my life.

They would buy a house much closer as the kids got older and then I visited more often. I actually lived in her attic for a short period of time while between residents.

Apparently both of my sisters loved kids and had big hearts. Dixie was taking in troubled foster children and I'm talking little criminals here. As for Melody, well her husband agreed to take in foster kids as well. They ended up taking in an entire family of three girls so that they wouldn't have to be separated.

Melody's was a mad house with the kids running around and her husband was a saint. She wasn't much of a housekeeper but she loved those kids and her family. Not sure how it came about but she was also counseling an older teenage boy and his then to be girlfriend at the time. She was doing everything she could to keep them in high school.

On any given night or weekend they could all be there. Which is why I stayed in the attic for just a few weeks, the noise and commotion were more than I could handle. My visits didn't last very long either once I moved out as I'm not a big kid's guy.

It was a couple years later that I met my wife Cynthia and discovered what a close family dynamic would look like. Not that they didn't have family problems but at least they were close knit and had close relatives as well.

Before I unfold more about her family let me finish with mine. For those of you living in the 70's and possibly in the Boston area you might remember a little snow storm called the "Blizzard of 78". Melody was pregnant with her 3rd child and was due that week. I was in a back brace after compressing a disc in my back at work and was being sedated to keep the pain done, Valium and Secanol (not sure of spelling) to keep me comfortable. I was Mr. mellow. It was the start of my back problems as maybe surgery should have been the answer, but I hated hospitals.

The weather men had predicted a snow storm starting in the morning and developing throughout the day. They had no idea of how much snow we were about to get or how fast.

I'm telling this story as a slight frame of reference so please bear with me and possibly enjoy a laugh. I lived with three friends whom had all gone to work. Another friend who was the brother of one of my roommates and also a good friend was coming over that morning to keep me company. His name was Bob and he was laid off at the time.

When I awoke that morning he was out in his truck and hadn't come in because he didn't want to wake me. I was in a lot of pain and not sleeping well which he knew but yelled at him for not coming in. The snow was falling quite heavily at the time.

I already mentioned the "Love, Sex and Marriage" and will add "drugs and rock-n-roll later, which friends and I were indulging in all quite freely at the time. Cynthia and I were planning to get married in the spring of 79, so I was enjoying all three now as well. To further set the stage our musical interests were the Rolling Stones, Doors, Black Sabbath and a couple newer bands the Cars and Queen.

Talk about naïve it wasn't until a Queen concert that I learned about gay people. It was drag queen central. Nothing like standing at a urinal with a guy in dress standing in the next urinal, I didn't care their music was great. I had a very care free attitude back then and thought people should just live their lives and enjoy them. I still feel that way, as life is too short as it is.

One of my favorite songs was "Live for Today" by the Grass Roots. I truly was living in the moment in those days. The pot smoking helped keep the mood as well.

OK I'm rambling big time here so back to the blizzard. By noon time it was clear we were getting a lot of snow. Of course Bob and I were listening to music, smoking pot, drinking and playing "pitch" (a card game) so we weren't getting any weather updates. It wasn't until his brother John (Mac) came home from work with one of his lady friends that we became aware of how serious the snow was and how bad the roads were.

Not being complete cavemen we turned the TV on and caught the bad news about the weather. The storm was bad, highways were closing from all the traffic and you should stay in once you got home.

Mac was my best friend and would be best man at my wedding. He was also a ladies man and was seeing quite a variety of them at the time. Back then most everyone in our circle had nicknames and this girl was no exception. She was Jewish and her father did not approve of Mac. Anyway he called her "The Jew". Please no hate mail; believe it or not it was a term of endearment in some crazy way.

One of the things he would say to her when we were discussing doing something or going somewhere was "I don't know would Jew" and then look at her. Did I mention she was a babe with a great body to boot, just painting the picture? Bob whose nickname was "Backseater" long story and I were toasted (state of mind) to say the least. Not sure why but Mac decided to take her home so she wouldn't get stranded at the house.

She was not happy and tried to change his mind with a trip to the bedroom. Even though we heard some moaning coming from his room for a short period of time they emerged and he drove her home. She lived across town and it took him almost 2 hours to get home. The roads were brutal. We fired up the blender and a few other things and played 3 way Pitch.

We got over 3 feet of snow that day and our other two roommates did not make it home that night. A driving ban had been put into effect and everyone was to stay home. Getting back to the original part of the story my sister's street was totally blocked and she was about to pop that baby.

Knowing Melody she was calling the city every few hours to get her street plowed so she could get to the hospital when the time came. They must have thought she was kidding or just couldn't get there until a few days later. The road was cleared when she went into labor and off to the hospital they went.

I honestly don't remember the phone call or who it was that called, but Melody delivered a beautiful baby girl and the baby was in good health. Mr. Naïve, why wouldn't the baby be healthy, then came the "but". My sister had shot a blood clot to her brain and was in a coma. This was the late 70's women delivered kids all the time with no problems. Heck she had already delivered two kids, I was in shock. Cynthia tried to explain how there could be complications with pregnancies and child birth, but this was my sister.

Without going into a lot of details I had found out a few months earlier that the baby was not her husbands. They had some crazy arrangement regarding her seeking other sexual gratification and she had become pregnant from a younger man. The younger man was totally in love with her and both he and my brother-in-law were devastated. The brother-in-law's family was appalled at the situation once they found out, as in his mother. Hitler had nothing on this woman, she was hard core strict.

As it turns out my father was not happy with Melody's choice either. At the time he was living in Florida. He did not come up for the funeral, nor did my sister Dixie. It was shocking to all and Cynthia couldn't fathom how our father and sister could not attend that funeral for Melody. That was when she truly understood I did not come from a close family.

Again I honestly don't remember all the details, but my sister Dixie adopted the baby girl. Her name was Angela and she raised her as her own. All these years later she still lives with my sister. I have not seen her since she was born. As for Melody's other two children I stayed in touch for a few years especially around Christmas.

Cynthia and I were married and a couple years later had our first daughter Jacquelyn and I let them just drift away from my life as did they me. Even though I left out a lot of details I think you can understand that family was not a big thing for me from a young age.

Then I would be introduced to Cynthia's Italian family. She had three older brothers, many cousins with Aunts and Uncles to boot. They got together every holiday. She talked to her mother pretty much every day. An older brother had gotten married and started a family when she was very young again no details but I was told no shot guns were allowed. It was a different time back then.

Her dad helped pay his family and college bills as he went through Med school. Being a family member now I was privy to some of the family conversations. After his graduation their mother referred to him as "my son the Dr." It wasn't long after that Cynthia and her other two brothers referred to him the same way, only it was "Ma's son the DR."

Like my older sister he too moved out of state. Like my sister he had separated himself from the family circle. Don't get me wrong he kept in touch with the parents and came for visits. Like me with Dixie, Cynthia did not know him that well and they were and are not very close. Again no details let's just say you can pick your friends not relatives.

On the bright side she is very close with her other two brothers and talks with them fairly regularly. As for me I call Dixie once in a while. We got together in Vegas a few years back so Cynthia could meet her. They had some long talks about my family and Cynthia now has a better understanding of where I came from.

We also had taken the family to California for a vacation and hooked up with her biological daughter whose name happens to be Melody and her daughters. So my kids got to meet a couple cousins from my side of the family. No they do not stay in touch after the one visit, go figure.

Sadly I have never met her adopted daughter Stephanie (sorry if I misspelled the name). Nor have I seen her son Robbie since their visit when I was younger. I am told he is a minister with a nice family now. Steph as my sister refers to her also has a nice family.

Earlier I wrote about "Marriage" and mentioned the divorce rate. At this time let me update how it relates to my family situation. I know it's kind of off the track but it does relate to family.

My youngest daughter CJ has been divorced and does not keep in touch with that family at all, has a child out of wedlock and is now married again and pregnant with their soon to be son. Her husband also has a son from another marriage. Jacquelyn married no plans of kids and her husband is divorced with two teenage children a girl and boy. She used to joke he had baggage when they were first going out.

Dixie finally did get a divorce. Her daughter Melody has also been divorced. Yes we are below the 50% rate and hopefully can stay there. After all you have to have lows and highs for an average.

Now let's take a short look at my wife's immediate family and will withhold names as they already know the facts. Cynthia and I are still happily married, did I say that, only kidding Pookie.

Of her three brothers, one has been married longer than Cynthia and I and they are still going strong. Both are retired and seem to be happier than ever, both of them are great people and I really enjoy their company. They have a beautiful daughter who is getting married this summer.

Here's where that average thing comes into play with the other two brothers. One divorced, remarried to a woman who was also divorced with children. They have been together much longer than his first marriage.

The other brother who happens to be closest to my age has been divorced twice. He married his High School sweetheart, but it didn't work out. After that he became a lot like my friend "Mac" and became what we now call a Player. Many girlfriends but it took a while before he remarried.

He too has a beautiful daughter who happens to be graduating High School this spring. Just a thought but I don't think he will remarry again. In my opinion he got taken to the cleaners twice as he truly loved both women and they were the ones that filed for divorce. I know it takes two to tango, but sometimes one isn't that good a dancer apparently.

So there you have it, two different family dynamics. I have no idea how my parents felt about Dixie's divorce. I did notice that Cynthia's parents were very upset with their son's. They supported both boys as best they could. As for my sister's, it just wasn't talked about. Again one of my favorite states of mind "ignorance is bliss" keeps me going.

Just as another point of reference regarding my train of thought about things, here is something my wife points out about my problem solving techniques. If I can't solve a problem or wrap my head around the problem so to speak then I ignore it. She says Jacquelyn tends to do the same and says it's a "Robbins" thing. As for me I ignore that train of thought and joke that I need to see a DNA test regarding Jacquelyn and the "Robbins" thing. I offer the same argument when CJ does something her mother refers to as my traits.

Denial is a great river did I mention I swim in it often. Not sure spilling the beans about the family was the best thing to do, but it sure makes me feel better. Who knows maybe some of you readers will relate. On the brighter side maybe more of you will appreciate your families a little more.

Hopefully you also understand why I like to add a little <u>fun</u> and humor to my "dys<u>fun</u>ctional" family. As for the laughter being the best medicine thing, I don't agree as I have a long list of medications I take daily. I will say the humor helps make the medicine go down. No spoon full of sugar as I'm a diabetic.

As for any of my living relatives that read this book and don't agree or like my family evaluation, you're all free to write your own book.

11

VACATIONS, WE ALL
NEED SOME FUN

D on't worry I'm not going to write about every vacation
I ever took, well maybe a few. As it turned out Cynthia
and I both had the same vacation experiences growing up. As
in getting in the car and driving somewhere, stopping for a
night then getting back in car next day and driving somewhere
else. We never stayed in the same place two nights in a row and
neither did her family.

Visiting relatives for a long weekend was not considered a
vacation, just something we did at least once a year. We were not
campers as my mother liked to have a solid roof over her head
with a nice warm shower. She also felt if she had to cook and
clean up afterwards it wasn't much of a vacation. Cynthia feels
the same way as my mother on this point.

I will say we tried the camping thing one time. We rented a
cottage in Maine with another couple and our children, one of
which was a baby. Looking back a few years later we agreed it
wasn't our best of ideas. The sun shined bright as we drove to the
lake our cottage was on. Sadly a couple hours after we arrived,
the sun decided to leave.

I had never seen so much rain for so long a time. By midweek with the forecast being for more rain Cynthia and I decided to take the family home and let the other couple and their family enjoy the cottage. I admit having a big case of cabin fever and was not enjoying myself at all. We took a nice drive around the lake and agreed the vacation was not being very relaxing at all.

Sometime the next day the clouds broke and the weather turned nice for the other family. I mention this change of weather as it proved a point that was developing involving my wife and vacations. It seems no matter what time of year or where ever we went the rain would appear.

We were lucky enough to buy a house a few months before our wedding so our honeymoon was a drive to upper New Hampshire as money was tight. This is when the pattern started to develop as it was rainy and overcast for the entire week of our honeymoon. Leaving us to just eat and well you get the picture it was our honeymoon. I had taken many vacations with friends before marrying my wife and had never seen such miserable weather.

Our next vacation would be Florida to see my Dad. He was telling us about the drought they were in when he picked us up at the airport. Later that night the rain started. It rained off and on the whole week we were there. My father thought it was amazing that they got so much rain while we were there. Myself I was beginning to think I had married a rainmaker.

This pattern would continue for many years. No matter where we went within a day the rain would arrive. It was uncanny Maine, Cape Cod, Florida a few more times it didn't matter where we went the bad weather appeared. We actually flew to the Bahamas' on a trip booked with a travel agency in late February one year for a summer type getaway.

It turned out to be the coldest week they had experienced in years and of course there was rain. The locals were wearing winter coats and we had brought only summer clothes with us. The hotel ran out of blankets for the rooms as they had no heat in any rooms and at night it got quite cold. There was a pool and nobody was going in it. We took a trip to the beach and nobody was going in the water there either.

I'm not exaggerating, it was a brutal week weather wise and the locals were stunned. Finally on our next to last day the sun came out and we had a nice outdoor day. We went to the beach again because I was determined to go swimming since we had gone there for a summer type vacation. I was the only person to go in the water.

No kidding people were pointing at me and laughing. Later that afternoon back at the hotel they were having a pool party. Once again nobody was in the pool just doing a lot of drinking and dancing. After a couple daiquiris' I dove in the pool, again this was supposed to be a summer like vacation. Happily a few other people jumped in, but not many.

This was the clincher; my wife was definitely some type of weather jinx regarding vacations. When her brothers were planning vacations they would ask Cynthia about our vacation plans to make sure they didn't plan theirs for the same week as us. They did it jokingly, but I noticed they were never on vacation the same week as us.

It happened so often that I thought we should offer to fly her to areas in the country that were having drought problems. I figured we could make some money on this phenomenon. You think I'm kidding, but I took her to Las Vegas, where my buddy was living. He was talking about how little it rained there and Cynthia was safe to come out and not affect the weather.

It rained the entire next day. He thanked her for the rain and never mentioned the weather again that trip, true story. On the bright side my wife is not a big fan of Vegas so I get to go visit on my own. It has never rained when I was there on my own.

Some years later she went back with me and we met my sister Dixie and her husband. She was excited to finally be meeting my sister after all those years. When I let my buddy know we were coming he joked about needing the rain.

We had to plan the trip for late August to accommodate our schedules. Cynthia was not looking forward to the 100 degree plus weather, but it's a dry heat, ha ha. The forecast was for sunny days with temperatures over 110 degrees with no rain in sight. On the second day that no rain in sight thing came to an end as it rained all afternoon. The weathermen there called it a freak storm. The money I could have made if I could have bet on that rain.

I had joked to my sister about bringing a rain coat because of Cynthia's past history. She laughed and didn't bring one; neither did we even though we knew better thinking it couldn't happen twice. Again my friend thanked her for the rain and we never talked about it the rest of the vacation.

I'm happy to say after the Maine vacation our family vacations got much better weather wise. They weren't rain free by any means, but we did see more sun than rain on most of them.

Let me get back on the subject and away from the rain thing. Since neither of us really didn't go anywhere on our family vacations as kids we decided that we would take our children places. The theme became amusement parks in our kids early years. Since I had taken Cynthia to Disney in Florida she knew our kids would love it there. Thus it was our destination for several vacations as our kids grew up.

At one point her parents had a winter home in Florida and my father lived there as well. Thus we had places to stay giving us more money for the parks. Each time we went we visited

Disney, Universal and Busch Gardens along with a few days at the beach. Our girls loved it and we could go out at night and leave them with the grandparents, a real win-win.

Both lived on the Gulf side as did our good friend Karen. So we spent most of the time in the Tampa area. Before I was married my friends and I would always go to Daytona Beach as well as visiting my dad in Clearwater. You just don't see beaches like that anywhere else.

The girls were just as impressed as I was about actually parking the car out on the beach sand close to the water at Daytona. I had told them stories about it but they needed to see it to believe it. For those of you that have been there you know what I mean. You can actually drive along the beach, no road.

A lesson I learned on my first trip on the beach is that you park alongside everyone else in the softer sand. When the tide is out that hard sand looks inviting to park on, however the tide comes in quickly. A long walk on the beach or a stop to play volleyball or a cold drink at the bar and you can come back to see the waves crashing on your windshield.

Your car sinks in the sand up to the floor boards and you have to wait for the tide to go out to have your car towed. It's a funny thing to see as long as it doesn't happen to you. I wonder how long it took for the interior to dry out and get rid of the saltwater smell in the car.

No it didn't happen to me, but I was lucky enough to see someone else's car being swallowed up by the ocean water. When we first saw the car parked there we thought they had a smart idea. A couple hours later when we walked back to our car we saw why it wasn't. We felt bad for the owner of the car, but we couldn't help laughing our butts off.

If you have had some crazy things happen to you and became the brunt of others laughter and jokes you know how nice it feels to laugh at someone else's expense. It's one of those things that really aren't funny but you can't help but laugh.

Trust me I have given many people things to laugh at throughout my life so it's nice when the laugh is on someone else. Remember those golfing stories I was talking about. Anyway vacations are for fun and laughter right?

Happily our family vacations shared those embarrassing moments and events for each of us. Like our youngest daughter CJ getting slimed at Nickelodeon while visiting Universal Studio's in Florida. She had joked about it happening to her but never thought it would. It was a highlight for her and the whole family got a great laugh.

Let's not forget the family river ride that Cynthia reluctantly took with us at one of the parks. She really didn't want to get wet so of course the first wave soaked her. The four of us were laughing the entire ride. Shortly after Cynthia got drenched so did CJ and I. Jacquelyn was laughing even harder at us as she was dry throughout most of the ride. I say most as right at the end the raft was going under an overhang and people were there with water guns squirting passengers as they went by.

Jacquelyn was bragging how dry she was when they opened fire on her. Talk about a surprised look. After the ride we spent a few minutes squirting other passengers going by. It was just as much fun if not more than the ride. All three girls thought it was great that they could get someone else wet that they didn't even know. I noticed that most everyone that got squirted went to the walkway to squirt someone else. At one point the line for the water guns was longer than for the actual ride.

For those of you that have taken your kids to these parks you know that there are height restrictions for some of the rides. Although our youngest CJ was the daredevil she could not get on all the rides when she was young. It was at one of those rides at the Six Flags in New Jersey where a strange thing happened.

CJ and I walked over to a game and I let her play while Cynthia and Jacquelyn went on this swinging boat type ride that eventually went completely around in a circle. What we jokingly referred to as a lunch loser. The game however was simple; they gave you several small rings which you tried to throw over the top of a bottle. There were a bunch of bottles on the table and you needed to get the ring completely around the bottle neck.

I bought a couple dollars' worth of rings and CJ started throwing them. She came close a couple times but it was harder than it looked. When she got down to her last ring she gave it to me to give it a try. I honestly don't know how it happened but I tossed it towards the table and it went right onto a bottle.

CJ was jumping up and down and cheering as though she had done it, I just looked in disbelief. What made it even better was we got to pick any prize on the stand. It was like hitting the jackpot. We decided on this 20 foot long white snake. While we waited for our prize the ride ended and Jac and Cynthia came walking over.

Cynthia looked a little pale and CJ was telling them both what had happened. As fun as it seemed at the time I had to carry that snake wrapped up in a plastic bag around the park with me the rest of the day. I can't tell you how many people stopped us to ask where we got it and then how we got it.

The guy running the game had told me they give out one every couple weeks and I was pretty lucky. It was one of those driving vacations and I hadn't thought about how much room it would take up in the car. I literally took it out of the bag and circled it completely around the interior of the car and back around to the arm rest in the middle of the driver's seat. On the plus side it also served as a barrier separating the two girls in the back seat. It became quite the conversation piece for years to come. We placed it downstairs in the playroom and it survived for many years.

Another amusement type vacation took us to Virginia. We visited King's Dominion, Busch European style, Water Country, Virginia Beach (where we ate lunch looking out at wild dolphins swimming off shore) and climaxing with a drive along the shoreline to a ferry over to Atlantic City. We spent a night at a casino then drove home the next day.

The Amusement park theme faded and we started going to places like Niagra Falls, then over to Toronto. We did the tourist thing at the Falls. As usual we had a rainy/torrential downpour day while there. Drove over to Toronto and stayed at the Skydome.

I had great tickets to a Blue Jays/Royals game. We visited a Wax Museum, played some miniature golf. It was a totally different vacation and the girls weren't thrilled when it was over. We had some fun, but it wasn't like the Amusement parks. The ball game was not a highlight for the girls even though they saw the Dome close. For the record it was a great game. A guy from the Royals hit 3 home runs, one near us and a player stole home. Again the girls will tell you about the Dome closing and nothing else.

The big vacation was still to come. I spent a lot of time online but put together a 3 stop master piece, I thought. Fly to California (LAX) via a 2 hour stopover in Chicago. Our first flight had a delay and we had to run through the Chicago airport to catch our connecting flight. They actually held the plane for us and everyone knew the Robbins family. Happy to say nobody was rude to us, not sure the delay was that long for them.

The plane actually picked up some time along the way and arrived ON TIME so I felt a little vindicated. Sadly our luggage did not make the connecting flight. As the groans started we were told it was on the next flight that was arriving in about an hour. We had lunch, my daughters got to see some strange looking people walking the airport at LAX. We lived in the country so the people watching became a lot of fun for them. My advice was to be respectful and hold back the laughter. Bald people dressed as Monks, guys and girls with spiked Mohawk haircuts with orange and purple hair, there was some sights to laugh at for sure.

We checked in for a rental car and got the luggage and off to the motel. Here's when the fun really started as our motel was across the street from Disney. It was 3 PM and we were checked in and had our suitcases in the room. The park was opened to 11 PM so I dragged the family across the street. I made a point to see all the exhibits and rides that were not in Florida.

What could have been a disastrous day turned into a great day. We spent another day at Universal and caught an Angels night game at their new ballpark. I had gotten the tickets from a salesman at work and they came with restaurant passes. The tickets were behind home plate in the balcony.

The girls were moaning about the baseball game until I reminded them they may see some TV Stars at dinner. We didn't but it seemed to smooth things over at the time. The food was good and Jacquelyn got her first taste of Crème Brule, it has become her favorite dessert. We were enjoying the atmosphere in the restaurant so much we watched the first two innings on the TV's there.

Let me share a pet peeve I have developed and that is not being late to anything. Even though we were at the game we were late getting to our seats. When we finally did get to our seats I would be greeted with a surprise. The guy sitting next to me had a foul ball which had landed in the seat I would have been sitting in the previous inning. It would have been a great addition to the vacation story had I caught it, but we did enjoy those desserts.

We met my niece and her family one afternoon and evening so the girls could meet some members of my side of the family. We also spent a day at Universal Studios. I probably have the order a bit mixed up after Disney, but you get the picture we were doing and seeing things so all was good. Next stop would be a drive to the San Diego Zoo for stop number two.

This stop did not get the positive response from the family I was hoping for and some of their best exhibits were closed for repairs. We arrived in the morning had a quick bite to eat and then went through the Zoo. My family will tell you I ran them through as quickly as possible because I wanted to get on the road for stop number three. I plead the fifth, as stop number three was Vegas and I had reservations at the new MGM casino the next day.

As I drove along they were discussing where to stop to eat and or spend the night. During the drive we had to stop on the highway as the police were checking all cars on the road. Nothing serious just checking for illegal aliens, one of my daughters was concerned about them until I explained they meant people coming up from Mexico. I will not divulge the name of the daughter who thought the aliens were from outer space. My wife blamed that on me for all the Star Wars I let her watch growing up.

If you have ever taken that drive you know it's mostly desert and not many rest areas with food and lodging. We did find a place to eat and I will not give out the name because it was the worst food we had ever eaten while on vacation. Somewhere along the way the girls had made a bet amongst themselves that I wouldn't stop until we got to Vegas.

At this time I will disclose I have a tendency to agree to stop along the way when driving on vacation to eat and or sleep so the drive will be broken up a bit. Sadly history would show I never stopped overnight and food was a very quick stop, mostly fast food when I could pull it off. Hey I'm a guy and like to get where I'm going, did I mention this time it was VEGAS.

So when we entered Nevada my wife called the MGM to see if we could check in a day early. No problem, they were glad to have us, not sure the look I was getting from the girls was a sign of agreement. I talked ice cream when we got their and the dirty looks subsided. Yes I did buy them ice creams after we settled into the room it was $18 for three, but hey I was now in Vegas.

At the time Vegas was trying to advertise itself as a family destination. The MGM had a small amusement park which is why we stayed there. It was also the new casino and the website advertised many family things to do. What it didn't mention was that some of them were not finished or opened. Happily the park was and it sported about 6 rides. It took less than two hours to do them all, some twice.

They did serve alcohol which helped my wife get through the last ride. No, she and I did not go on the ride, but the girls thought it would be fun. It was a slingshot type ride that brought the two of them up in a harness some God knows how high and they are released to slingshot across the park a few hundred feet in the air and go back and forth until they bring them down.

While they were getting prepared to go on the ride Cynthia and I got a couple of tall Pina Colada's to watch from below. As they were bringing the girls up to the release point it dawned on my wife that her babies were up there and she got a bit panicky. By that I mean freaking out as she inhaled her drink like it was water and her mouth was on fire. She was holding my hand at the time and was literally cutting off the circulation from squeezing so hard. I assured her they would be fine the ride was safe and here, have some of my drink.

The instructions they gave the girls were simple, when ready pull the cord and they would be released to slingshot across the park. As I said earlier CJ was the daredevil of the group and immediately pulled the cord. Needless to say her sister wasn't ready which added to the screaming. Being their parents we could recognize the screaming as they flew by us overhead. CJ's screams were of joy and Jacquelyn's of fear.

The ride ended and they both came running over joking about how fast CJ pulled the cord. They commented on how pale their mother looked and no they wouldn't be doing the ride again. My hand was released and the girls got a big hug from their mother and I went back for another drink as mine had mysteriously disappeared.

Other than the daily show at Circus Circus and the ride at the top of the Stratosphere (which only CJ went on) there was not much else for the kids to do. I will mention my wife went to the top with CJ and Jacquelyn and I stayed on the ground floor. I'm not big on heights, although I will fly to save time. They serve alcohol at airports and in planes so that can be comforting.

Another day the wife took the girls to the M&M factory, the Elvis museum and a few other places I can't remember along with some shopping. I went gambling with a buddy of mine. Needless to say the wife and girls were not impressed with this part of the vacation.

Jacquelyn and CJ did do one other thing together while we were there and that was going to an evening movie. Cynthia dropped them off and then went back and picked them up. While waiting to pick them up an attendant walked up to Cynthia and asked if he could help her as she looked lost. She explained she was picking up her kids and was just waiting.

He immediately told her our two daughters would be out in a couple minutes as the movie they were seeing was almost over. I'm sure my wife's jaw had dropped open so he continued by explaining they were the only two people in the movie as it was PG. He went on to say that it wasn't uncommon for the movie to run with no audience as adults didn't watch PG movies in Vegas.

That would turn out to be our last whole family vacation. It seems once you graduate High School going on vacation with Ma and Dad is a no-no. We did take CJ to Florida one more time where another strange thing happened. Let me start by saying it wasn't uncommon for us to run into people we knew while on vacation. By that I mean no matter where we went on family vacations we met someone we knew.

Let me also point out that I planned most of the vacations. I booked the plane tickets and found hotels to stay at. On this particular vacation we spent a few days with our friend Karen along with a couple days on both Clearwater and Daytona Beach. Karen setup our stay at Clearwater and I took care of Daytona.

My criteria for Daytona was rather simple, I wanted a hotel on the beach with an outdoor pool overlooking said beach. It also needed to have a bar that served alcoholic beverages. As you can imagine there were a few to choose from and I had no trouble getting reservations. Neither I nor anybody we knew had ever stayed there. You will understand that statement shortly.

I'm happy to say the weather was perfect for the beach and we spent the first day going from the pool to the ocean. It turned out to be everything I had been looking for all in one. At the end of the day we had a nice supper and went back to our room. Since CJ was only 16 we rented her a movie to watch on TV and Cynthia and I went down to the bar.

I'm told being from the Boston area that we have an accent. It must be true as whenever we go south people ask us if we are from Boston. After ordering a couple drinks the bartender asked that same question, "Are you from Boston"? Having heard this question many times the wife and I said yes and she went on to explain how closely we lived and grew up in the Boston area.

Somewhere along the conversation I told him I grew up in Quincy but had moved to Weymouth as a teenager. These are two suburbs south of Boston which I didn't expect him to know. So here is the conversation that followed as I recall it.

Bartender "Where in Weymouth"? I answered North Weymouth.

Bartender "Where in North Weymouth"? I answered Blackstone Rd.

Bartender "What number on Blackstone Rd"? Before answering I looked at him real close and was sure I didn't know him. Not knowing where this line of questioning was going I told him 49.

He stuck out his hand to shake mine and informed me he had been my next door neighbor on Blackstone Rd. He had been a small boy at the time which was why I didn't recognize him. Talk about a small world. My first job ever had been working for his father installing and servicing burglar alarms. I was the go-fer.

Another crazy fact to the story is that his dad got me into drinking my coffee black. His reasoning was are you drinking coffee for the taste or for the cream and sugar many people add. I will not mention any names, but he will know who he is if he reads this as his son called him from the bar that night and told him I was there. Let me also thank him now as he helped instill a good work ethic within me and showed me the way an employee should treat his boss and customers.

Oh heck Ken if you read this thank you and I hope you and your wife Rose are doing well.

The wife and I took a cruise for our 25th anniversary. It island hopped around the Bahama's. Cynthia will tell you she really enjoyed it and would definitely do it again, but it will not be with me. Let me just say it wasn't my kind of vacation and leave it at that.

Anyway as a family we had some nice vacations and we did get to visit some interesting locations. Since both Cynthia and I were blue collar workers at the time there was a trade off in taking these vacations. That trade off was not having a college fund for the girls. We made it clear if they wanted to go to college they would need scholarships or attend a state school which we could afford.

I bring this trade off thing up as I'm sure it happens to many families in similar positions as we found ourselves. Some might say it was selfish on our parts to take the vacations, but in the long run the girls still talk about some of those vacations.

As for college, Jacquelyn took a year off then went back to school part time. Once she got within a year of her degree she quit working and went to school full time. I'm proud to say she got her degree at Bridgewater State College in marketing. As for CJ she tried attending the same college on two different occasions but life got in her way. She is now married with a 6 year old daughter and a son on the way.

Growing up we would have thought CJ would be the college grad as she loved to read and had great grades going into high school. Jacquelyn was more the social butterfly. She did have a drive to get things she wanted and once college got in her sights she went for it.

Getting back to the vacation theme, Cynthia was lucky enough to take a trip to Italy the year before we were married. She is 100% Italian and her parents still had relatives there. It was her last family vacation before getting married and starting our family. The guest list included her mother and father (who could still talk and understand some Italian), brother Phil and his lovely wife Cathy and brother Steven.

As beautiful as the pictures and slides were I will never go overseas. This will probably sound crazy but there is just too much more of the good old USA for me to see before venturing overseas. Having a "bucket list" has become a popular subject for discussion since the movie came out. It might be boring but my list consists of visiting places within our great country.

The fact that I don't travel well anymore is another reason for not going overseas. Lately I have trouble with a car ride over an hour long. Even if I don't get to see any other places in the USA, I grew up in New England and did get to see quite a bit of it over the years.

Cape Cod was just an hour away by car throughout my entire life. Although I don't get the allure some people have regarding its beaches and sights, it is a nice place to visit. I must say we saw one of the most interesting 4th of July parades ever during a visit to Provincetown. They do things a little different at that far end of the Cape. There is even a clothing optional beach or two in that area. If interested just ask a local as they know the best spots.

My family was from Maine so I spent a few weeks visiting Aunts during my summer vacations. I mentioned those driving vacations where we ventured through Vermont and New Hampshire. In the summer time my dad would take us swimming at some of the beaches in Rhode Island. The waves were bigger there and we could do some body surfing.

As I write this I realize we never went anywhere in Connecticut. However I was stationed at the submarine base in New London for over a year. Servicemen weren't much for sightseeing, but we did find our fair share of bars.

I almost forgot the resort/beach vacation we took with another couple to Punto Cana. It was a beach with a couple bars and some interesting food choices. It was a vacation spot for Europeans as well. I mention that as most of the women who went topless at the pool and beaches were not from the USA.

By the way when they advise you not to drink the water that includes ice cubes, I made a point not to drink the water, but was having ice in my Sambuca. It was a 6 day trip and I spent one in the bathroom, I'll spare the details. When the gentleman from the other couple started with the same symptoms' the night before we were leaving the ladies pointed out the ice thing with our shots of hard alcohol was probably the cause. They said they felt bad but they still laughed at our expense. Looking back I was lucky to have gotten sick in midweek as the other gentleman was still feeling the effects when we went to the airport to fly home.

I'm purposely leaving out the other couples names so to protect the innocent so to speak, but their friends will recognize the story. The short version is that he couldn't stop going to the bathroom and when we got to the airport all the stalls were full with a waiting line. As badly as he was pleading no one would give up their stall. Apparently most of the men were using the ice cubes as well.

About a half hour went by and he still hadn't come out of the bathroom so his wife sent me in to see how he was as the plane was starting to board. I found him cowering behind a trash barrel and he informed me he needed a change of pants and underwear. Like I said no one was giving up their stall and he couldn't hold it any longer.

As embarrassing as it was for him I had to go out and tell his wife he needed a change of clothes, let the laughter begin. As I said they were loading the plane and our luggage was already aboard. She had the task of asking one of the baggage attendants who barely spoke English to let her go into the baggage compartment of the plane and get some clothes for her husband. I'm guessing this wasn't the first time this had happened since he escorted her to the back of the plane while telling all the other attendants. They were really getting a kick out of it.

If this wasn't embarrassing enough she could only find her bag with her clothes in it. After a few minutes she came back literally crying from laughter and handed me a pair of women's white pants to bring in the bathroom for her husband. It was a small airport but I'm guessing most of the workers had heard about the mishap as they were lined up outside the bathroom as we came out. Did I mention the pants were kind of see through in the bright light of day.

To his credit he handled it admirably as the three of us laughed and joked about it during both flights. Yes we had a stopover, which he had to suffer through as well.

Needless to say we weren't being very subtle about his predicament and several of the other passengers were starting to chuckle about the situation. A couple months later we brought him a box of Depends when we went to his daughter's High School graduation. There was a whole new group of people who knew the story and were heckling him.

Well that's how Cynthia and I decided to handle family vacations. Both girls still got the opportunity to go to college even though it wasn't as a live in experience. Best of all we didn't go broke making it happen and really did get to enjoy those vacations. Like marriage, doing things within the family was a compromise and work in progress. The daughters may have wanted more of a say in those destination vacations, but I pulled the "my money my final choice card".

I still have tee shirts from some of those vacations and when I wear them I can and do reminisce about them. I should mention

I try to find a good tee shirt everywhere we go along with a shot glass. It's just been a tradition I started when we were first married and went on our honeymoon.

As we are getting closer to retirement age Cynthia and I took a couple trips to states we would consider retiring too. The first was Nashville/Memphis, both were great for visiting but sadly some of the locals frowned on more "yankees" moving into their residence. They didn't seem to understand that people from Boston were insulted to be called a "yankee", it's a baseball thing. As nice as the areas were they had a strange tax structure which wasn't geared towards retiree's.

Being an Elvis fan I enjoyed Graceland and Beal St in Memphis was interesting to visit as well. The natives just weren't that friendly. For example while sitting in a bar listening to some "blues" on Beal St the gentleman sitting beside recognized my Boston accent and berated me and my wife for being northerners. He wasn't being overly rude just making a point that "southerners" would prefer we visited and not move down there.

If I had been 30 years younger I may have pressed the issue a bit as some of the comments were getting to be a bit rude. Instead I asked him how long he had lived in the area? When he answered 15 years and he had moved down from Maine I started laughing. Cynthia and I finished our drinks and got up to leave. He wanted to know what I was laughing at and with a straight face I said "It was a northern thing". Cynthia grabbed my hand and semi pulled me out the door.

As we walked down the street she started laughing as well. The idea that he had moved there from further north than we were living and he felt accepted there but we would not was just ironic. After walking about a block we stopped and Cynthia asked "you were about to insult his intelligence weren't you"?

Still chuckling I told her I wasn't sure he would have recognized the insult. I honestly can't tell you what great line I planned to dazzle him with, but looking back I'm glad we left.

In the few minutes we sat near each other at the bar I had learned he was jobless and about to lose his place of residence. Yet here he sat in the middle of the afternoon on a weekday drinking instead of looking for a job. He had a couple empties in front of him when I sat down and you could tell he had been drinking a bit. So yeah I had a nice zinger for him although I can't remember it and it was a good thing to as I was in my fifties and him thirties, which was why the wife hustled me out.

Back to the vacation thing, we also made a couple trips to the Charlotte area. Beautiful country and people there and they didn't seem to mind where we came from. After enjoying out first visit we went down again to look at houses and or land lots. Besides the people being nice they didn't get much snow which is a big plus for the wife and I. We have both lived in New England for over 50 years and the winters are getting a bit tiresome.

Anyway North Carolina is a great state to visit with many places to tour and activities to enjoy besides the nice weather. If my lower back had not deteriorated ruining my mobility we probably would have retired there. As for the people we met there, well they didn't seem to mind we were northerners.

Another fun fact about the state is they are turning some of their tobacco farms into vineyards. We visited two and I can tell you they are definitely on to something as their wines are very good.

12

PARENTING/FATHERHOOD
A WORK IN PROGRESS

Having and raising children is a huge responsibility and shouldn't be taken lightly. During our engagement and early years of marriage Cynthia and I had many discussions about the issue. We both felt firmly about planned parenthood, thus I did what most men do in this situation and left the birth control in her charge. This will not be a popular statement for the mothers/women reading this, but I knew Cynthia would be doing most of the work when the children were young so I wanted her to be ready and sure before starting a family. How's that for a saving grace come back?

To prepare us for childhood we decided to get a dog shortly after we were married. Not that we were comparing children to dogs, but there was a responsibility level with both. You know start small and work your way up. Thus we got Charlie, a Lhasa Apsua (not sure of spelling) a small very hairy dog with an attitude. Charlie would prove to be more like a child than we expected.

Shortly after he arrived home with us he stopped eating dog food. After a couple days of not eating Cynthia did what any mother would do and started cooking for him, mostly eggs and hamburger. No joke the Vet had told her the dog would eventually eat dog food, but after a couple days she cracked.

My wife would take the dog to work with her as she owned her own seamstress shop. Occasionally she would stop at MacDonald's for breakfast and of course Charlie would get an egg-McMuffin. It didn't take us long to realize we were catering to the dog, again a good comparison to children.

Just to let you know how bad it had gotten here's a quick story. A friend was on his way over to visit and asked if we needed anything at the store since he was coming over. Cynthia asked if he could stop at MacDonald's and pick up a cheeseburger and small fries. He laughed saying it wasn't much food and she told him it was for the dog. Needless to say he thought she was kidding until she actually started breaking the cheeseburger up into Charlie's bowl.

Our friend looked a little shocked, so Cynthia explained the reason she was breaking the cheeseburger up in the bowl was because if she gave the dog the fries first then he wouldn't eat the burger. You must admit that is something smaller children try to do as well. He could not believe she was giving the dog the food and stated we were crazy to spoil the dog like that. I agreed and blamed Cynthia for the whole situation, which is what any father would do if his child did something out of the ordinary.

One more thing about Charlie was he hated the mailman, who slid our mail through the slot on the door. He would literally stand on the other side of the door and growl, snap, bark and jump up and grab the mail as it came through the slot. He would make a point to bite every piece of mail that came through the slot and spread it down the hall.

Back in those days you had to send your bills back with a check to whomever you owed the money too. I'm guessing the bill collectors got quite a laugh as ours would always come back with teeth marks or partially chewed up.

Sadly the dog developed a skin disorder and the medication drove him mad literally. One morning I awoke to him growling and snapping at me and he chased me out of the bedroom. When it was obvious he wasn't calming down Cynthia and I agreed to call animal control and have him removed from the house.

So you would think having the questionable dog experience we would have decided against having children right? Somehow we convinced ourselves that children would be much easier to handle, after all we had been kids. Looking back that logic was insane. On the bright side having Charlie did give us some insight into the kind of strange problems small children can present you.

Jacquelyn is our first daughter; she came out crying and sadly kept that up for months. When the nurse and I walked her to where all the babies were sleeping her crying literally woke them all up. The nurses were not happy and I got some brutal looks from them as they tried to quite all the babies down. Alas Jac was a colicky baby and it lasted for almost 6 months. It was a very trying time for new parents and my mother-in-law did a lot of baby watching during those months to help relief the strain.

As years went on we would discover that she had Colitis and as a teenager had to have part of her colon removed. At different times throughout her childhood she would have to spend weeks at a time in the hospital. I'll spare the details but it was a tough time for the whole family.

On the bright side Jacquelyn was always a head strong child. Once you started doing something with her a few times it would become a routine with her. At the age of two we began watching Dr. Who on the PBS channel. It was corny sci-fi but she loved to watch it with me. For those not familiar with the show the Dr. was a time traveler and regenerated every few years.

It was a British show and he traveled in a police box and had several different female companions throughout the series. Jacquelyn liked the first Dr., who was played by a Mr. Baker, when he regenerated to another person she was a very unhappy camper. We continued watching for a short period of time, but she never warmed up to the new Dr. so we stopped watching.

A few Christmas's ago she actually found a DVD with the old Dr. and we sat and watched a few episodes. I could not believe how cheesy and phony the special effects had been. Looking back neither of us could understand what we actually liked about the show.

I must confess I used the TV and VCR a lot to help babysit when I was watching her. I know it's not babysitting when they are your kids, but I'm a guy and that's how we see it. (No hate mail please). Strawberry Shortcake was a life saver for me as she watched the same tape three or four times in a row. When she was older about seven I think I sat her down on a Saturday morning and had her watch the Star Wars Trilogy. Today they are known as episodes 4-6.

It was a great babysitter at the time and she loved them. Sadly she is 32 now and still obsessed with the entire 6 episodes. From time to time she will have weekends where she has friends over and they watch 4-6 on Saturday and then 1-3 on Sunday. Who knew I was creating an obsession for her.

You would not believe how much memorabilia she has documenting the different Star Wars episodes. Myself I like to collect the villains' just to be a little contrary. Jacquelyn actually had a Star Wars themed wedding a few years back. Have I mentioned her husband is a saint for putting up with her?

Anyway back to the parenting thing as I haven't actually given you any insight as to how we were raising our children.

Here's the thing, I was the baby of the family and had no idea how to take care of a baby. Being a boy I did not do any babysitting the way many teenage girls do while growing up. I was a clean slate so to speak.

However I did watch Wild Kingdom, which was on just before Dr. Who so I did learn how different animals raised their young. I know not the greatest of comparisons', although I have heard parents refer to their children as animals and little monsters. Cynthia had done a lot of babysitting growing up and her mother was wonderful with babies, after all she brought up four children. The other three were older brothers, as Cynthia was the baby of her family as well.

Again I had a lot of confidence that Cynthia would know what to do and together we should be able to figure it out. I consider myself a rather logical person, so I tend to analyze problems and situations as they present themselves through life. So basically I was clueless about how to raise a child. Being a guy I did know that there would be a lot of lovemaking/sexual activity in the process of getting Cynthia pregnant. I was right about that one.

As it turns out the idea of getting pregnant when you are planning for it can be quite the turn on for women. Not only do they get to enjoy the activity but it also is serving a purpose. Thus we developed the term going at it like Banshees. I had no idea how Banshees went at it, but for us it meant multiple times throughout the day and night. Yes those were good times.

We didn't have many hard and fast rules for our children other than using manners and having good behavior. Again we tried to teach those good values and the importance of an education. As they got older there were curfews for bed or going out, you know the normal parenting stuff.

As for discipline we did not belief in spanking, although an occasional swat on the butt for continual bad behavior happened from time to time. There were no time outs in those days; it was "GO TO YOUR ROOM YOUNG LADY". Sadly our first child Jacquelyn was what I would call a "work in progress".

Other than her health problems I mentioned earlier she was what many called a handful. She was headstrong at an early age and still exhibits that quality as an adult. Thankfully her husband gets to deal with that now, did I mention he's a great guy and I talk very highly of him since he has to deal with her now. Johnny good luck buddy, I got your back but she's all yours.

Daughter number two, Carolyn J (no name just initial) had and still has a totally different personality. We tried to keep the basic rules the same, but had to adjust on the fly when other problems arose. Our thinking was we could handle anything after Jacquelyn, we got a rude awakening when C J became a teenager. From a personality stand point you would never know they were sisters.

As a father I tried to encourage sports, but the girls didn't go for it. Both tried Gymnastics when they were young, but neither stuck with it. I had Jacquelyn try tennis for an 8 week session after which she informed me it wasn't for her. She did play volleyball in high school. Myself, I considered that a cookout sport; please no hate mail for my ignorant position on the sport.

C J did the horse riding thing for a couple years, but then got bored with it. She was a cheerleader for one year. She just never found anything she liked to do for any period of time other than reading. To this day she still does a lot of reading and no, it didn't lead to great grades in school, however she did work at a bookstore for a few years.

I know this will be kind of a cliché, but my philosophy was trying to keep the rules simple and straight forward, with little gray areas. As with many things I do I try to use the KISS rule whenever possible (keep it simple stupid).

Looking back I think Cynthia and I did a nice job with both of them. Happily they both graduated High School, one is a college grad and both are now married, ye huh.

As the girls went through their teenage years Cynthia's philosophy was to "chose her battles". Another way of putting it was not sweating the small stuff. All parents know that those teenage years are tough. Happily they got better for us. I can truly say that both girls would consider their mother to be their best friend and not many days go by that they don't talk and or text her.

As for my relationship with them, well it's a bit like I have with their mother. You know, a lot of head shaking and those familiar words "really dad are you kidding me". They know my style and humor and tend not to be amused with either most of the time.

For those of you who watch NCIS you know the main character Gibbs has "rules". My family will tell you so do I and they are not written down. I call them habits from 60 years of living and how I do things or in today's lingo "how I roll". Like I wrote earlier they consider me a piece of work, which I consider to be a good thing? I now have a Granddaughter who also does her fair share of head shaking and rolling her eyes at me. Nothing like getting a lecture from a 6 year old, hands on hips and even some foot tapping, I find myself asking "who's the adult here"?

To my knowledge there are no classes you can take like Parenting 101. There are many books on the subject, but they are mostly other parent's opinions or ideas. I'm sure some have college degrees or teach the subject and some may even have children. Heck not to change the subject too much, but I had a female professor who was teaching a class called "Divorcé and the Family" in college. Her credentials were that of being divorced 3 times, no mention of children.

The thing I discovered was when parenting there were many wrong ways to handle things, you needed to find those positive ways that worked for both you and your child. I had daughters who liked to argue with me, thus my logic to a situation or problem would make them stop and think (sadly not for long). When they were younger the point was we were the adults and what we said went. As they got older that argument went to the wayside and there was more communication and dialogue.

No matter what the problem or situation arouse both Cynthia and I would try to have a solution which involved our main concerns. Yes we made some compromises, but somewhere in there our concerns were addressed.

Most parents look back and think about things they may have been able to do differently. Heck that's the way life tends to be about everything. As for me, well I tend to be a little more simplistic about my daughter's.

To my knowledge neither girl is a serial killer or mass murder. They both are married and happy in their situations. Best of all, THEY DON'T LIVE AT HOME. So I will grade my wives parenting skills as an A+ and mine at a C. Like Biology I tried, it just wasn't my best subject.

I just reread the chapter and realize it's a bit light on parenting tips. There is a big reason for that. Please don't laugh but parenting is like the place people from all over visit, thus there are many ways to get there. Most parents are just trying to do the best they can for their children. We all come from different backgrounds, education, financial levels and family upbringing.

Cynthia and I took our experiences growing up through life and tried to take the best and shift through the not so best. No one has all positives as they grow up and go through life. Money may make the quality of life a little better, but it doesn't mean children growing up in that environment become better adults.

You know that old saying about leading a horse to water but can't make him drink. The same goes with teaching values and manners to children. Sadly the best parenting doesn't always lead to great results. As parents you do the best you can and hope your children understand and recognize right from wrong, good from bad and what it takes to be a good person.

Wouldn't it be easy if there were a set of steadfast rules and guidelines that would lead our parenting to a positive result with all our children? Sadly there isn't. One thing I did learn was to praise the good as often as possible and try not to dwell on the bad. Rubbing your child's face in his mistakes is not a positive reinforcement and it can lead to them shutting you off. I will leave this point with this, how do you handle constant negativity at work, with friends or at home?

The defense or in this case parenting/fatherhood bantering comes to a rest. I hope these insights help, even if it's what not to do. Again I get a "C" for fatherhood; it's the wife with the "A".

13

I'M A GUY AS I'VE
MENTIONED EARLIER

No snickering, "guys" tend to have what I call universal traits. That women are from Venus, men are from another planet thing is more biological than environmental. Without going through all these medical breakthroughs, a woman needs something from a man to have a baby. A man needs women to have babies to carry on the species. It sounds a little animalistic but its how most species normally survive without the help of science. Simply put "guys" are crude and tend to be unrefined. Gentlemen and most men have control of their inner guy, but let me share these thoughts with you on the subject; after all I've mentioned the "guy" thing a few times already.

Men are physically and mentally different from women (for guys that mental thing can be a wide gap). Within that difference are chemicals which change our bodies and thoughts accordingly. Being a guy I will try to use my KISS method to explain my point and deliver some facts. Sorry guys but I'm also about to let the cat out of the bag on a few issues as well. We all develop at different rates and ages so please, be flexible with my age examples.

As children growing up boys and girls look a lot alike with clothes on, until the Beatle era when boys' hair started to be as long as or longer than some girls the length of hair was a dead giveaway. I was taught to respect girls and not play as rough with them as I would another boy. Some of these girls were bigger than I was, but my father made the message very clear. His last point being I would understand when I got older. Let me clarify, that understanding was they were different not that I would understand girls/women in general.

Becoming a teenager means many things to both girls and boys. It can be summed up by "puberty", although that doesn't cover the whole change. Girl's bodies go through visible changes as does their chemical makeup. The same can be said for boys noting a change in voice to a lower tone. Let's not forget that hair grows in places it hadn't in the past for both.

I'm not going to go through all the biological changes and chemical changes let's just say guys notice girls for more than just friends to play with after school and vice-versa. It can be a cruel time as attractions are formed and not always reciprocated by the opposite sex. You know just because I like or are attracted to you doesn't mean you are to me. The point is like it or not boys are now looking at girls in another way. This is also where some of those "guy" traits develop.

Again all boys look at girls and this continues as they grow up to be young men and look at young women. The reasons may not be completely clear in the early years of puberty and may change as we get older, but it is still a fact, even if it's just out of curiosity because the girls are starting to look different from the boys.

This is the time when boys begin "checking out girls". Yes I mean all boys. As young men sexuality kicks in, but young "guys" are still looking at women, it might just be for different reasons. Go anywhere you want and do some people watching and you will find all types of men (old, young, gay, straight, transgender or other to cover the varieties not mentioned) and you will notice them checking out the females in the vicinity. We the guys may not be looking at women for the same reason but trust me we are still looking at them.

Here's a little secret to share with the women out there, most men can find at least one positive/attractive trait about you during their checking out stage. We all come in different shapes and sizes with a variety of looks, but men find positive features in almost any women, and that's before they even talk to you.

At this time I will share a trait I find to be very positive with any women I encounter, that is their wearing a dress or skirt. No matter their looks, size or disposition, I find this type of attire to be feminine and it gives me the feeling that they embrace that aspect of who they are. I'm not trying to come off as a male chauvinist pig, I'm a guy. Don't shoot the messenger; this is my point of view.

To clarify a little further or dig my grave a little deeper depending on how people are looking at my point of view, this type of attire on a woman will always bring me to look at her a bit longer. Don't get me wrong I think women in general are attractive and tend to dress themselves nicely when they go out in public. It's just my opinion but a woman in a dress or skirt is looking to be recognized as an attractive women and not just an attractive person. I just reread that and I'm not sure it's the point I'm trying to make, but again I'm just a guy.

Let me change the subject a bit and look at how a gay man might look at a woman. Again my opinion, it would be more of a hair/makeup/ what the hell is she wearing that for type of look. Is my grave getting deeper? The point I'm trying to make and probably doing quite badly is they are still looking at women.

There are many cliché's surrounding women's beauties, and of course I will use one that will probably help to dig my grave on the subject. I'm cleaning it up a bit but here is the gist of it "find me a beautiful women and I will find you a man who's tired of making love to her". Here's my biggest problem with that statement, it suggests that all the man was interested in was the woman's beauty.

Thus my point that all women are beautiful, but it can be in many ways. How's that for a recovery?

Back to the guy thing, more of us than care to admit are borderline lecherous voyeurs when it comes to women, we just try not to make it too obvious. The rest are gay or in some stage of denial (there's that grave again). Remember the opinions expressed in this book are mine and developed through my 60 years of living on this planet as a guy.

Let me digress to my first couple years in Junior High. The age was 13-14 years old and I knew nothing about sex or girls in general, still not much about girls/women. I was the true definition of naïve. I had no idea what was happening to my body or why certain things would happen to me. One of those things that were happening way too often was the lump I was getting in the front of my pants from time to time. The same sensation I had when I woke up in the morning minus the pants, yes an erection. Is the guy thing starting to come across? This is a very embarrassing time for a teenage boy.

It was becoming a bit more frequent, as it was happening a lot in school. After getting a nasty head shake from a female teacher who noticed my lump I decided to ask my father about it. He was not ready for the bird and bees talk yet so his advice was to untuck my shirt so that it covered the front of my pants. If a teacher asked me to tuck it back in, ask to go to the bathroom so I could tuck it in with some privacy. It was some of the best advice he ever gave me growing up and yes my shirt went untucked a lot.

As I grew older and began dating I would find that the girls I dated liked the fact that I would need to have my shirt untucked around them, especially after I told them why. Yes I was discreet about the explanation. I had inadvertently stumbled across a great pickup line that worked for years. It was also true which was a double plus.

Before changing the subject from women let me throw out a few scientific observations regarding males and sex. No I can't name them but I'm sure you've heard the points I'm about to make on the subject. Teenage boys think about sex quite a bit and those thoughts dwindle in frequency as they get older but at a slow rate. That being said, isn't it a good thing that those thoughts are about women or in the case of a gay male a man instead of something destructive or harmful?

I can see the hate mail/email coming from everywhere after those comments, good thing I won't be running for public office. With everything that's on TV these days I'm guessing most women realize my comments about guys are not that far off. Yes there are exceptions for better or for worse, like marriage ouch.

So let's move on to how we guys like to make decisions as we go through life. Again the KISS principle can make things very easy. For me I'm always trying to find a simple and logical answer to the problems that come up as I go through life. This will sound real simple, but I eat foods I like and avoid those I don't. The same with people, I try to be around those I enjoy and avoid those I don't.

I am my own person and behave accordingly. I have developed a fashion style that tends to embarrass my kids and that my wife tolerates. I will clarify this style by telling you I own over 30 pair of gray knee socks and they are the only socks I wear no matter what the occasion or attire I'm wearing with them.

I have always liked the feel of socks going over my calves and now it's all I wear. Since they are all the same color and length it's easy to match them up during the folding process of laundry. If a sock develops a hole I don't need to throw the pair out only that sock, then just wait for another sock to develop a hole and throw that one out leaving me with another pair. I can never have two different colored socks on as all of them are gray. Unlike my granddaughter who seems to always have two different socks on.

I wear these socks with and to everything, weddings, and funerals with shorts no event or outfit has an exception. My golfing buddies gave me the nickname "Socks" as I wore them all the time no matter what color my shorts happened to be. I do not go barefoot or wear sandals. The wearing of my gray knee socks is a "rule" and one I haven't broken in many years. Yes I do get the occasional strange look when I'm walking around in shorts and sneakers. My daughters and wife call this a "guy" thing although they don't know any others that wear them all the time.

On the bright side there is not much of my leg exposed while out in the sun so I don't get any bad sunburn on my legs. The socks thing is my fashion statement and staple so to speak that I have made and kept with through my latter years of life. For other guys it could be worn out hats, jeans, tee-shirts or something they just can't part with or stop doing. In this case the guy thing is the quirk or attachment women don't get.

Guys do things that women just don't understand even things that they know aren't good for them. One that jumps to mind is having a few too many cocktails. We tend to let the good time over rule common sense and spend the next day suffering from the bad decision. Sorry ladies but age doesn't always stop this behavior, just makes it less frequent. Cynthia will attest we have had our worst arguments/fights when I have had a few too many. I'll plead the fifth on that one, as in the fifth I should have stopped drinking.

Guys watch a lot of sports especially football. College football starts the last week of August and with playoffs and the Superbowl goes into February. Exhibition football takes up the month of August for the diehards. ESPN talks football all year round nowadays.

As I wrote in my sports chapter we have it 24/7. Women aren't worried about losing their man to another women, it's the sports channels that are becoming their biggest concerns. So here it comes ladies, if your guy is a sport nut you can feel pretty confident you're his one and only women. The reasoning is simple he doesn't have time for you, sports and a mistress.

Sadly the flip side for those whose husbands aren't obsessed with sports, what are they thinking about or doing in their spare time since it isn't sports? If they aren't watching sports on the internet why do they spend so much time on it? I feel like I may have just ratted out a different group of guys.

All men are different and have various degree of guy in them. How much they show or let out depends on them or the good woman they've found to tolerate them. By a women's standard there may only be a few good men out there, but trust me there are plenty of guys.

Guys are crude which is why men need to understand when they can be the "guy" and when to be the cultured man. Here's a great example, I tend to pass gas (fart) or burp when the urge arises. Depending on who or where I am will depend on how much I try to conceal the release of said gas. I don't know why but shopping especially the grocery store seems to bring this function out in me. Sadly I can't control the noise made during this passing, which is usually the giveaway to my wife. At which point I get the stern look, asked why I couldn't hold it and of course the push down the aisle. In defense of my action I tell her it's better to bare the shame than the pain, like there's much pain. When that doesn't work I just tell her the truth "hey I'm a guy".

By now I would like to think that I have made my point. Just a thought, but it's possible that men who don't marry or are divorced not looking to remarry may just have too much guy that they let out. Remember ladies, you need to be careful when you ask a man to just be himself.

Not that the guy thing has any defense, but I've met some very crude women in my time that show some of these traits. I'll let the women define their behavior as I can get in enough trouble on my own with the opposite sex. Just a reminder I have a wife, two daughters, a granddaughter and three female dachshunds. Needless to say I have my share of interaction with the opposite sex at several different levels.

My granddaughter, Lily Harmony has no problem putting the guy in me in its place. She's strong willed, stubborn and I call her "bossy Betty" when she gets a little pushy. She will also joke about her "gas passing".

As for the dogs they don't mind the guy thing as long as they get their food and treats when they are supposed to. Like me they can be a bit crude and they have no problem barking or passing gas whenever the urge strikes them. Now that I think of it maybe that's why I've heard women refer to men as dogs from time to time.

Another thing I've noticed is they get away with a lot more of the behavior I get criticized and lectured about. Even Lily gives them less lectures than she does me. Again nothing like a lecture from a 5/6 year old girl to put a guy in his place and Lily has the body language (foot tapping and arms folded) down to a tee.

To end the chapter on a positive note, remember ladies you need us guys if for nothing more than to compare your man to us. We also bring some comic relief to your lives even if it's just friends or acquaintances'.

14

MOVIES WE'VE COME
A LONG WAY BABY

Through 60 years of living I have watched a lot of movies and find that I still enjoy them. I have my favorites and have watched some movies more times than I care to admit. I will state upfront I do not like or watch horror movies. When I was younger I was lucky enough to see some of the great movie star legends bring to life movies about, Dracula, Frankenstein, The Mummy and of course Wolfman.

Forgive the spelling but Bela Legosi and Vincent Price were house hold names. Throw in Alfred Hitchcock as a director and you have the early pioneers of horror and the bazaar. You look back at those movies now and the acting and props were terrible compared to what they can do today. It also had less violence and gore. Again I wasn't a fan so I will keep my opinions to myself since I haven't seen enough for a true judgment.

Give me a good comedy or action adventure anytime; I don't even care if I know the actors or actresses starring in the movie. I enjoy being entertained. That's not to say I don't have favorites in either category. I found Mel Brooke's movies a must see when I was younger.

Blazing Saddles is one of those movies I find myself watching a lot. However, it needs to be the uncut version to really bring out some of the best jokes and lines. If you are familiar with the movie then you know what I mean. If you haven't seen the uncut version take the time to watch it, you will get a great laugh.

Young Frankenstein rates right up there as well. Gene Wilder starred in both, but Teri Garr may have stolen the show in Young Frankenstein. Those familiar with this movie can still chuckle thinking about the ride from the train station to the castle adding a dose of Marty Feldman and those large eyes. Remember these lines "walk this way" and "what a nice set of knockers". I still use both of them from time to time, how's that for the "guy" showing up in me.

My wife enjoys both movies as well and may have gotten one of the bigger laughs from the people around us when she used one of those lines. Let me share the story quickly even though I caught the brunt of the joke.

We had toured a couple of the mansions in Newport, Rhode Island with our good friend Karen who was visiting from Florida. The walking had taken its toll on my back and hip and I was starting to show a definite limp. Cynthia wanted ice cream, so as we drove home we were looking for a place to stop. There were several Newport Creameries in the area and I was sure there would be one before we left Newport. I went by a couple other places and the ladies were starting to give me a hard time about my not stopping.

They were just getting into their heckling of me when we came across one to stop at. They both wanted the ice cream but I sensed they were disappointed we came across one and the heckling had to stop. I parked in a handicapped spot as I have a flag to do so. Then proceeded to enter through the wrong door and walk much further than I needed too. I was definitely feeling the pain from all that walking during the tours.

Anyway we ate our ice cream and started for the door. Between the driving, walking, driving again and then sitting to eat the ice cream my back had become very stiff and I was walking awkwardly as we headed for the door to leave. Cynthia jumped on this opportunity to utter "walk this way" and started mimicking my limping towards the door. There wasn't a lot of people in the place but as I turned back to say something to Cynthia they all started laughing. She was dragging her leg behind her just like Igor did in Young Frankenstein.

Both Karen and Cynthia laughed and joked about that for most of the ride home. I have to admit the timing was great everyone including the waiting staff got quite the laugh out of it. So there is a nice example of how a movie was able to brighten peoples' day just from remembering that scene. It was at my expense literally as I think I paid for the ice cream as well. That's what I expect movies to do for me, entertain me while I watch and later when I'm thinking about them. It's nice to be able to use a line from a popular movie and make people laugh while doing so. Laughing helps me go through life as I've mentioned earlier.

Another great comedy actor in my opinion is Richard Dreyfuss, although he's probably best known for his role in Jaws. Check out "Let It Ride", if you haven't seen it his mind dialogue is hilarious. Teri Garr plays his wife and a young Jennifer Tilley does a great job supporting as well. Don't let the title fool you as the laughs just keep on flowing. I've found as I watch this and the other two movies I mentioned that I know the lines before they are said and I still laugh.

Personally I'm not big with some of the slapstick humor that goes around today. I was a Three Stooges fan back in the day, but some things just can't be recaptured. Don't get me wrong Jim Carrey has made some funny films as "Liar Liar" comes to mind. The pet detective movies had some funny lines as well. There's just something about those first three movies that set them apart from other comedies.

When talking comedy the uncut version of Animal House rates right up there at the top. Being 60 I can relate with many of the movies old stereo types. Accept the movies female nudity for the situation's that they appear and tolerate the colorful language in that same context and just enjoy the laughter.

As for action adventure, the "James Bond" movies really have a nice flow to them. Daniel Craig has really updated that character. Sean Connery was the true ladies' man/ secret agent. Roger Moore added a bit more comedy to the role. Pierce Brosnan brought together a little of both. As for the other actors who tried to play the role, well they didn't cut it for me. Don't get me wrong I enjoyed most of the movies, but I prefer to watch those four actors when I watch one of the movies again.

That being said I'm still undecided about the latest version, Skyfall. I will definitely need to see it again before ranking near the bottom of the list. It didn't seem to have the same action scenes as the others. The special effects tend to make these movies worth watching. The plots can be a little weak as can be the supporting cast, although each movie likes to introduce the new "bond girl".

Ursula Andress coming out of the water in Dr. No might be the best "guy" scene for the bond classics involving the female costars. As womanizing as these movies were and still tend to be, I don't recall any real nudity. Everything was an innuendo or slight glimpse to leave the rest to the viewer's imagination.

They have their share of violence and explosions, but not much blood. They have their own place in the action adventure category.

After watching Skyfall again last night sadly it stays at the bottom. On the bright side the end opened up for some new characters with renewed old names. You'll have to watch it to see what I mean as I will not be giving that observation out.

I grew up with John Wayne and must say he still carries the honors for his Western style movies. Clint Eastwood ranks second, but his other works far surpass his westerns. Wayne didn't only play a cowboy in his career, but that is clearly the role he gets remembered for doing. How many of you remember or have seen the comedy Son of Paleface?

It starred Roy Rogers, a very famous cowboy actor with a supporting cast of Bob Hope for your comedy relief and Jane Russell (what a bombshell) as the female lead. Don't forget Roy's horse "Trigger" who has a very funny seen with Bob and a blanket. Trust me it's worth watching for the laughs and the trio's version of the song "Buttons and Bows".

I still recite some of those lyrics and taught them to my granddaughter. "I was peaches, I was cream, I was captain of the team" and she replies "I like soap and I like water makes me smell just like I otta". Watch the movie and enjoy the laughs, remember it's old and the special effects are a bit lacking. Bob Hope really knew how to deliver a line and his facial expressions will crack you up as well.

The movies of today have unbelievable special effects. The overall quality of the acting has also improved immensely. I admit my older movies tend to lack in these departments, but they were great for their time.

Here's a recent movie I've watched a few times recently, Trouble with the Curve. Clint Eastwood takes the lead, but is not the most compelling character for me. It has a baseball theme, although I'm not sure I would classify it as a "sports" movie. Check it out as my wife has watched it numerous times as well.

As for movies in general they have a 20 to 30 minute window to get my attention and interest, my wife feels the same way. As she puts it "something has to grab you", if not it gets shut off. We have friends that disagree and tell us about movies that pick it up as they go along. Yes we have gone back and given a few movies a longer view, but I can't think of any we watched to the end.

When we were younger before VHS and DVD's we actually went to the movies. Myself I got tired of the crowd noise, advertisements and cost of snacks so I prefer to watch at home. We have walked out of movies within that 30 minute window shaking our heads over the money we just wasted. Let me tell you when you have invested more money than time into a movie and you can't stand to watch it any longer, then it really isn't doing it for you.

Blue Lagoon was one of those movies. We were vacationing on Martha's Vineyard and had spent most of the day at the beach. It was a clothing optional beach and almost everyone was taking that option including us. We knew no one on the island. Being an island your entertainment at night was limited. To Cynthia's surprise and I'm sure a few other women's we would see many of those same people from the beach in line at the movies.

The running joke became would any of us recognize each other with our clothes on. The "guys" were very cool about it, but there were some red faced women in that line waiting to enter the theater. Who knew at the time that standing in line was going to be the highlight of the movie. We were not the only couple to leave the theater before the movie was ½ over.

If any of those reading this book remember that day and evening I hope you agree. The beach was the highlight and I thought all the women looked great (there's that guy thing again). As for Cynthia she enjoyed the voyeuristic side as well and found that being naked with strangers didn't bother her. However her face got a little red as well when some of the guys said hello to her as we stood in line.

If you have met my wife you would know why they recognized her and I kept telling her it wasn't the long red hair. It was what that hair was not covering up if you getting my drift, I'm sure the guys do.

Back to movies, I find it much more enjoyable to watch in the comforts of my own home. The price is right, the time is flexible and you can pause for a break (bathroom) without missing anything. Another great feature is REWIND in case you didn't understand or hear something correctly.

Both my daughter's and their husbands still enjoy going to the movies for the "big screen effect". As for myself I watched Return of the Jedi the day it was released while vacationing in Clearwater Florida. Cynthia stayed at my dad's house rather than watch that movie as she is not a Star Wars fan. Little did I know at the time I would not go to the movies again until the newer Star War movies were released.

Since breaking that drought I have gone to the movies with one or both daughters to see Episode 1, 2 and 3. Jacquelyn might be one of the biggest Star War geeks around. Her condo is literally filled with the movies memorabilia. No exaggeration she has even joined a couple of groups known as Comic-Con and Dragon-Con whose members thrive to meet the old and new stars from these and other type sci-fi movies. I'm just glad it's not plain Con, just kidding she's never been in any trouble in her life.

Most Halloween's she dresses up as one Star Wars character or another. She makes her husband do the same. She actually has become some type of officer from one of the groups and travels around the country for the different events. She is in Atlanta this Labor Day weekend.

The three of us also went to most of the Harry Potter movies for the big screen and sound effects. Yes I have read all the books at least twice, the earlier books four or five times as I would reread them before each movie or book release. Thus Star Wars and Harry Potter movies rule the sci-fi category for me.

I can't tell you the last time I went to the movies with my wife, but I'm guessing it was the early 80's. Yes she gives me a hard time about that, my response "sorry but you don't like sci-fi and that has the best overall big screen effect". To date that response has been enough although that probably won't last much longer.

It should be noted we have had a very large TV for many years to watch our DVD's on. We have had "surround sound" for many of those years as well. Can't say the dogs are big fans of the "surround sound" as they tend to look around the room for what is making the weird noises. They make their own noise if the TV has a barking dog.

Drive Me Crazy is another one of those movies I can't help but watch when it's on. Once again it has some great lines for its context as a teenage movie. When the boys are sitting at the side of the small waterfall and the girls are floating below on their plastic rafts, both parties talking about the other. One boy talking about closing the deal with a girl uttering those three magic words, only to get interrupted by the star with "another tequila shot". For me that was typical teenage boy banter.

So there you have my movie picks and why. To sum it up the way my granddaughter and wife would "seriously Grumpy that's what you're going with". Yes it is. It's safe to say I will never be asked to critique any movie or film for the public as my tastes are very narrow minded.

15

RANTS GET IT ALL OUT

Right now in this day and age there are some serious atrocities' going on around the world and I'm talking about the possible chemical weapons Syria used on their own people for starters. Several different countries spoke up and suggested some type of military action against the offenders. As usual they all backed down or backed off depending on your point of view and left the USA and the United Nations to sort it out. Has the U.N. ever actually intervened on anything?

Other countries felt they should be left to their own demise, how humanitarian of them. President Obama is asking Congress to evaluate and help determine if we should get involved. One big problem Congress is on vacation and its leader doesn't feel this is a strong enough issue to call them back early. Thus we will wait almost two weeks for them to reconvene and discuss the issues surrounding this matter. Don't expect any quick action there. Congress and politics in general has become a very slow process. The pace being slow or stopped.

I don't like seeing this country being the world police, but I do think Congress could cut the vacation a bit short and go back to Washington to hear the details. The previous President and his Congress were kind of quick to invade a Middle East country after 9/11. That was on American soil, but that country had nothing to do with it, just speculation that they had weapons of "mass" destruction and they may support terrorism. All I'm asking is come back from the vacation early and start some dialogue on the subject.

As we would learn later no weapons and the terrorists responsible were not there either. In this case we have living proof and it doesn't rate a little urgency? I just don't get it. We are talking CHEMICAL weapons used against human beings.

Here's another one for you, gun control. The President wants to tighten down some of the laws restricting the purchasing of a gun, especially semiautomatics and people are going nuts over it. The Pharmacy has stronger regulations for cold and allergy medicine. The laws are more strict for these or tobacco purchases than from a minor buying a gun, isn't the internet grand.

How many innocent children have to die before we tighten the requirements to purchase a weapon, especially by another child? Can we start using just a little common sense here? Our leaders invaded a country for trumped up reasons and yet we can't have tougher gun laws? The public shootings continue to happen, but its business as usual for gun control.

It is amazing how many things the government is allowed to regulate for a multitude of reasons, yet potentially saving a few lives with stiffer gun regulations isn't one of them. Sadly I'm afraid it will take a horrific act of gun violence against a politic group before we see a change. To date shooting a Congresswoman wasn't enough.

I know both issues I have just brought up are much more complicated than I made them out to be or are they? If we aren't going to help people whose own leaders used chemical weapons on them, then why help anyone? Sorry world USA is sticking its head in the sand and taking care of ourselves period. We have troops and embassies all over the world let's bring troops and people back and close them down. We'll figure out what to do with all those people and equipment later. That is how the government tends to work isn't it? You know jump then look. Case in point the new website for healthcare (I know low blow).

Instead of gun control put metal detectors up everywhere, if you set it off you don't go in, simple. As for the gun violence lets go back to the days when someone shot a member of your family you went and shot a member of theirs. It doesn't matter if either victim actually did something to the other family just an eye for an eye pure and simple. I hope this sounds ridiculous to all or most of you.

On the bright side this may slow down some of our immigration problems. The number of Americans looking for work would be astronomical leaving little room for immigrants to get work. Disagreements could be settled by shooting each other, thus giving us some population control.

These solutions might be a bit drastic, you think? Isn't there a saying about taking steps backward to go forward? I hope my sarcasm is at least giving my readers something to think about.

Let me add it's been a couple weeks since the chemical weapon incident and Congress came back in session. As with most political agenda's it appeared there was some flip-flopping of opinions. The result was to do nothing and let them figure it out. The country in question did agree to stop using the weapons.

As for gun control, a troubled young man opened fire at a Navy Yard outside Washington D.C., killing 12 people and he was shot dead to bring the total to 13. A rally is going to take place with the survivors of some of these shootings asking Washington to please do something more about gun control. I hope it's a nice day, otherwise the bad weather will add to their misery of our countries leaders doing nothing but giving them lip service.

Let me lighten the rants and look at the grocery stores. I don't know what happens to those nice mothers, grandmothers and people in general once they go through the doors of a grocery store. Some type of transformation happens, as many become rude, vulgar and completely disregard any form of courtesy. Let's not forget the manner in which they push their carts around the store as though they are the only ones there.

It's only been the last few years that I started accompanying my wife to do our grocery shopping. With the exception of what the items cost most of the stores are setup in the same manner. The aisles are wide enough for two carts to go down them in opposite directions just like a road. That fact only holds true if the carts are pushed along the sides of the aisles and not DOWN THE MIDDLE.

Not to sound petty but using the rules of the road in the aisles of a grocery store should not be a foreign concept. Let me also add if you don't allow your children to drive your car then they shouldn't be pushing your cart. I have been cutoff more times in the grocery store by a woman or her child pushing their cart with no regard to the shoppers around them than driving in rush hour traffic in Boston.

On the bright side they are just as rude if you bring it to their attention. I like to push our grocery cart through the store, it's kind of challenging. I have been bumped, slammed into, scolded, lectured, yelled at, sworn at and ignored after being cutoff and sadly that's just the first aisle. The produce aisle is like a war zone where you literally put your wellbeing and sanity to the test.

I have had fruit and vegetables taken (ripped) from my hands and told "I was looking at that" by the women grapping them from me. On one very weird day a women took a head of lettuce out of my cart because it was the last one and she really needed it. I stood there for several minutes in disbelief until my wife came over and asked me what I was doing. I told her and she laughed, then asked "where's the lettuce"? She didn't believe me until looking in the cart and actually seeing the lettuce missing.

I'm sorry ladies but I have never had a man in the grocery store be as rude to me as some of you have been. I can't remember the last time my wife and I went through an entire grocery shopping without some type of incident. Here's another of my favorites, having someone move my cart as I'm trying to put an item into it. Really you couldn't wait until I finished getting my item, then you give me the dirty look. I'm telling you something happens to women in a grocery store.

It's probably to save money, but what happened to stores stocking their shelves at night when the store is closed? Now many aisles have one or more pallets of cases that need to be sorted, opened and put on the shelves. To complete this action they need a person in the aisle actually doing the restock and they need some place to put the cases once emptied, usually one or more grocery carts.

These pallets just add to the congestion and traffic within the aisle. Not to mention they are usually blocking an item which I'm trying to get at. As with my road rage theory regarding turn signals, maybe these pallets have become the root cause for the bad behavior and ill manners throughout the grocery store. Like that theory maybe they just hit one too many pallets in an aisle and snapped. I know that sounds farfetched even to me.

Maybe the stores aren't circulating enough air. Whatever it is I'm sorry but many women change once in a grocery store. To put it in Star Wars lingo they turn to "the dark side". On the bright side I can happily report no serious injuries other than bruised ankles.

At Christmas my wife got a calendar featuring how people dressed at WalMart. I expect the next place for such a calendar will be the grocery store. It's amazing how people will dress to do their shopping. Sorry again ladies but you can go from beauty queen to street bum. The guys don't care what they are wearing as they are there for a purpose. As for the women they usually have a little more self-esteem about their appearance in public.

Let me share with you some of the fashion statements I have seen walking through the grocery stores. Pajamas have become a regular form of attire and not just the younger women wearing them. Sometimes they even have their bathrobes on with them. On a rare occasion I have seen the bathrobe covering some sort of night gown. In these cases the more flimsy the attire the more men seem to be following.

Bathing suits and not just one piece have been known to pass as grocery shopping worthy. Depending on how good looking the women is wearing them will determine how many guys are following them. I have seen several men get the rabbit punch from their wife's or girlfriends once they realize what is going on. Proudly I would like to state that Cynthia has never slugged me in the grocery store for that reason, just told me to stop drooling and keep moving.

Some rare sightings have been wedding gowns, bridal attire, Halloween costumes (at least I hope they were), ball gowns, lingerie showing through a scantily clothed covering, and the favorite of the guys the see through top with nothing on underneath. Those last two tend to have a male following throughout the store.

More common items are clothing that fits way to tight revealing what may or may not be on underneath. Definitely showing the curves of a women's body even if they are not very flattering, as in please put a long coat on. In the summer months shorts seem to be popular, most are tasteful and others suggest the woman is trolling for a mate.

By now I'm sure you get the picture and have seen a few yourselves, so let's move on to the checkout counters. A common complaint when the store is busy is there aren't enough registers open and you need to stand in line. I understand the frustration but these stores can't always predict when people will do their shopping. Managers have to schedule their employees work schedules and it is far from an exact science. Sorry but in this case we the shopper need to suck it up.

It's the "express" lines that torque my cookies. Stores vary as to how many items they allow in these lines. I have seen it vary from 8 to 16, although 10 tend to be the average, thus the sign "10 items or less". Yes you know where I'm going with this, 10 is the maximum number here.

Happily I very rarely find myself at this register. I will also choose a register far enough away so that I can't watch other people going through the express register. Sadly I have a hard time restraining myself from making a comment when I see someone go through the register blatantly over the 10 item amount. Sometimes the clerk will point it out to the patron in case they didn't read the sign, but they still usually check them out anyway. Giving the benefit of the doubt I will concede it could be an honest mistake sometimes, but you can tell when the person is just in a rush and doesn't want to wait in a longer line.

It's these times when myself control leaves me and I find myself muttering something about Math not being someone's best subject. Let the glares and rude comments commence. The glare tells me you know what you did and think I'm rude for pointing it out and yes I probably was at that. However once you make a comment then you have opened the door for dialogue and I will point out what register you are at and how many items I have countered that you are buying.

Trust me I only point out the blatant offenders and they never like my observations. Most of these conversations end with the offender suggesting I perform a sexual act on myself which I'm not limber enough to do. It's also the point where I shut up and shake my head, as I feel they got my point.

If Cynthia is with me during these exchanges then I will be getting a lecture once we get to the car and a rabbit punch to drive her point home. Her point as always, "keep your mouth shut and know that you were right and they were wrong". For those husbands out there you can understand the hypocrisy of my wife telling me to shut up and I will leave that one alone as I do love my wife and being married.

Final point there is no "gray" area with the sign "10 items or less". If you disagree with that statement then Math is not your only problem. It could just be you enjoy being a bit contrarian. As for me I just avoid the register, no sense putting myself in harm's way. For me this is what I call common sense.

Shall we move to the parking lot, see chapter on driving for some of my points in general? I have found that grocery stores have very organized parking lots. Fire lanes are clearly marked as are the handicapped parking spots. They have collection areas throughout the lot for you to leave your empty carriage once your groceries are in your car. Parking spaces are clearly marked and they usually have painted arrows showing which way you should be going in a particular aisle.

The point is they go out of their way to make your parking experience simple. So what's the problem? Your parking spaces are clearly marked, just put your vehicle between the lines. If you don't have a handicap tag or aren't a fire truck don't park or stop in those clearly marked areas.

Lastly walk your empty cart over to the designated area. When you don't it becomes someone else's problem. The store has people collect the carts from these areas on a regular basis. Sadly those people spend more time collecting stray carts than emptying the designated area. Are you really that busy or in such a hurry you can't walk an extra hundred feet round trip? Heck call it exercise, don't think of it as being the courtesy way of doing it.

People it's the little things that can make or break some other people's day. I know it sounds corny or even a bit petty, but how often do you try to pull into an empty parking spot only to find someone's empty cart? That nice easy spot now has an obstacle.

You can try to gently push it out of the way with your car. This solution can lead to other problems like hitting someone else's car with the cart. Get out of your car and physically move the cart to another location, hopefully the marked area. Both of those solutions have made that cart someone else's responsibility or problem. Or you could do what many people do and just park in another spot.

Being the rebel I tend to be, I have been known to park in a different spot and still move the cart to its rightful spot or even use it for my own shopping. After finishing loading my groceries into my vehicle I may actually take someone else's cart to the designated area along with mine if it's on my way. I can't help but imagine what would happen if more people took this rebellious approach, heaven forbid. Yes more sarcasm and hopefully you get the point.

We are not alone. A random good deed could actually come around to someone you know. This rebellious behavior of mine can be attributed to both the Cub Scout and Boy Scouts of America. Growing up I was a member of both even reaching Eagle Scout in the latter organization. I may not have retained many of their fine teachings, but one has stuck with me throughout. Try to do one good deed each day no matter how small. My favorite and probably the easiest, hold a door open for someone else entering or leaving the same building as myself. I have found over the years that I go that extra mile and say "have a nice day" as well. To date I have not been struck by lightning for this behavior. Most of the people I do this for will actually thank me and tell me to have a nice day as well, not all but most.

Truth be told, I have come to enjoy holding the doors open for other people. Is it possible I'm not really the "grumpy" old man my family believes me to be? I won't tell if you won't.

Back to the rants that pretty much covers the grocery store we all love to go too. Who knows maybe the people reading this book will look at the store from someone else's experience instead of their own. Let me warn you though, one good deed could lead to another.

Patience is not a virtue I have regarding professional appointments like a DR. or Dentist. I understand they are highly trained professionals in their field especially those specialist. Depending on how well they are recommended the waiting period to see them can be longer than others. This will also show in the waiting room as in crowded and running late with their appointments for that day.

Over the years I have adjusted to these situations and have made a few concessions. First when I arrive I would like to know how late the Dr. is running if at all. If the waiting room seems a bit crowded I will ask for this information. I would appreciate it if the person I asked doesn't miss lead me (lie seems harsh), so please be honest. Their answer and the urgency of my appointment will determine if I stay or ask to reschedule.

Some offices do not react well to my rescheduling request. A few have suggested it constituted a missed visit and comes with a monetary penalty. On those occasions I will offer to make the copay, but will still reschedule. As you can imagine this has led to some interesting conversations.

It's my opinion that by rescheduling I'm actually helping them get back on track with other appointments. History has shown me that if I start talking rescheduling and then don't I'm in for a longer wait than was first suggested. I suspect that happens on purpose at some of these appointments. I'm not one of those people who will give the receptionist a song and dance about my time schedule and expect to move up the waiting list.

Again I'm not looking for special treatment, but I find these waiting rooms to be very uncomfortable and at times stressful. I make it a point to arrive at my appointments a few minutes early for several reasons. First if I'm not on time why should they be and sometimes there is paperwork to fill out.

Here's what really goes up my spine so to speak. They are running a bit late and it's already after my appointment time and another patient comes in who had an earlier appointment than mine but they are running really late for it. Many offices allow this person into the exam room before me. I'm sorry but this person should have to wait their turn. Am I wrong with this thought process?

Over the years I have found that this happens at some of the offices I visit on a regular basis especially the Dentist. When having my teeth cleaned I will call about an hour ahead to see if they are running late and if so by how much time. If it's an hour or more I ask if it's alright to show up 45 minutes later than my appointment or they can reschedule me. Again my reschedule can help them get back on time with their appointments.

Sadly it is the Specialists that always tend to run late and I find I need to keep those appointments. Knowing it will be a longer uncomfortable wait I will adjust by taking some pain medication to ease the pain and stress.

Sadly my back specialist is never on time with my appointments and I suspect that I'm being black balled a bit because I pointed it out on several different occasions. I wasn't trying to be rude, but I thought the assisting nurses who check me into the exam room should know.

They definitely forgot about me during my first visit at their clinic as I wrote earlier I fell asleep on the exam table and when I woke up most of them were at lunch and those who weren't didn't know I was still there. Since then I have not had one appointment with the Dr., where he wasn't at least an hour behind.

My last appointment I told the nurse about previous visits and how I seemed to get lost in the shuffle. She assured me there were only TWO people ahead of me and that it would not be a long wait. I thanked her and added please don't forget me. My exam room was the middle of three and there was another across from me and they were empty when I went into mine. While waiting I heard the nurse check patients into all three.

Yes you know where I'm going with this, as the Dr. visited all three of the other rooms before mine. Although I actually went into my exam room on time I didn't see the DR. until over an hour later. Is it me or is something strange going on here?

Sadly I see this Dr. about once a month to have my pain medication refilled or updated depending on how I'm doing. Even my wife is starting to question why these appointments are taking so long, especially when I see the Dr. what seems to be a very short period of time during these appointments. My last appointment was at 10:15 and I didn't get home until noon. It's a twenty minute drive and I made no other stops, you do the math.

Now it's time to go off on the NFL (National Football League), which opened their season, on a Thursday night. Since they were using their Monday night format for the game they referred to the game as Monday night football even though it was Thursday. Cynthia hates all football but even she thought a multibillion dollar industry should know the day of the week. That will become her rallying cry for the year as she compared it to wrestling, pointing out they seem to know what day of the week it is for their events. The following week it was recognized as Thursday Night football.

As bone headed as that was, the week of pregame hype was even worse. There are TV stations that just cover sports and they over analyze games like this for a week before it's played. Many of these TV analyses are retired players and or coaches and not necessarily the better ones. Most of the rest are journalists, reporters or announcers that cover all sports with football being their favorite.

My point is that they give their opinion as to how they see the game being played and what they may expect from each team. Since many of them have been around the sport most of their lives I expect them to have some good insights. What ticks me off is when they all seem to miss the obvious. The opening night game they analyzed for a week was Baltimore Ravens (last year's Superbowl winner) at Denver Broncos which was one of the teams the Ravens beat during the playoffs.

For a quick off season summary, the Ravens lost 4 of their best defensive players including the captain and inspiration. They also lost their most consistent wide receiver during their playoff run. The Bronco's had added one of the best slot receivers' to their offense, but had lost a key defender who now played for the Ravens and had another key defender on suspension.

I know there are many other changes and factors that happen to teams in the off season, but those were the highlights for me as a fan and sports bettor. The analyst's somehow felt the Ravens had replaced those missing defenders with better personnel than they lost and they would be better than last year. Are you kidding me, this was a huge leap for me especially in week one. Football is a timing sport and players develop chemistry with playing with the same players.

As for Denver they felt the offense would be better but those two players lost on defense would affect their pass rush and give the Ravens an edge. Not to simplify this mathematically, but the defense losing 4 key players would adjust and be better than the team losing two? Seriously that is how they saw it.

Bottom line so to speak Denver was a 7-1/2 point favorite in Vegas where the professionals make the betting line. The TV analysis' felt it would be closer than that spread and if Denver could not find a pass rush with those two missing players then Baltimore would win the game outright.

They were right on for the first half as Ravens led 17-14 going into the half time. After the break Denver would out score Baltimore 35 to 13 and have FOUR quarterback sacks for the game. That slot receiver the Bronco's picked up scored 2 TD's and caught 9 of the 9 passes thrown to him. Final score 49 to 30, so maybe those 4 missing players had an effect on the Raven defense, you think? As for the Ravens offensive player they gave away for a 6th round draft pick, he caught 13 balls for over 200 yards receiving in his first game for another team.

Talk about so many "so called experts" missing the obvious. No wonder they didn't seem to pick up on the fact they were playing Monday night football on Thursday. It was only the first game of season so there is plenty of time for them to get better and actually notice the obvious. Hopefully they will at least get the day right and as mentioned they did.

By the way one of those retired defensive players for the Ravens joined the TV analyses. He felt their defense might be a work in progress and couldn't believe they gave that receiver away. I'm sure being recently retired his opinions about his old team couldn't be taken seriously, but they were spot on as it turned out.

So I don't lose too many female readers let me change the rant to a subject they know more about, school children. One of the scary facts surrounding many parents is that their children need to ride a school bus to and from school in many communities. Being a logical person I would expect the bus drivers would get a fair amount of scrutiny before handing them the keys to the bus and responsibility of our children.

I would also think there would be some hard and fast rules as to what their responsibilities were as well. Just my opinion but actually dropping the children off at the correct stop should rate rather high on that list. You know right up there with not being abusive and having a good driving record. Not to sound petty but speaking and understanding English might also be a strong job requirement.

So who do the parents blame when during the first two weeks of school a driver gets lost for over an hour and in his frustration verbally abuses the children then drops them off at the wrong stop? This happened in a Boston suburb the end of the first week. The schools response was that they fixed the problem and alerted the other drivers this should not happen again under any circumstances. Really, because sadly it happened last year in a local community and they said the same thing. Procedures have been put in place to keep this from happening again.

Am I missing something here or is the job requirement to pick children up at their bus stop then bring them to school. At end of day pick them up at school and bring them back TO THEIR STOP. This isn't something that should have a "gray" area to it. Somehow there was a big time communication breakdown and the driver is not the only person at fault.

This is not one of those cases where you don't excuse blame but fix the miscommunication. "Sorry had some bad communication, it shouldn't happen again". This is one of those should never ever happen scenarios'. Maybe I'm overreacting as both my daughters rode the bus and now my granddaughter is doing it.

Again where was the common sense here, your other state of mind? I classify these simpleton acts as "da" effects or "what the hell were you thinking if it all?" My wife and daughters know if I use the "da" word then something stupid just happened or was said and they are hoping they didn't do it.

When this story broke on the news, Cynthia's reaction was the same as mine, didn't this just happen last year? What happened to learning from your mistakes, especially when you're dealing with the education system? Our education leaders aren't exactly setting a stellar example in this case.

I'm sure I'm overreacting, what could possibly go wrong dropping young children in a neighborhood they aren't familiar with? After all it's not like we live in a world of crime or violence within our cities. Even the sarcasm is scary when you're talking about our children.

On the bright side our Congress was back and session and they discussed the Syria disturbance as I pointed out earlier. It was pointed out the Russian leader felt the same way as our own Congress. Nice to know our decision making is in good company.

I'm just glad they had the conversation. If only the budget talks could go as quickly and as well. It still bothers me that our country has such a hard time balancing a budget and actually having the parties agree that it needs to be balanced. My bank frowns when I go in the red or below ZERO with my checking account. Our country and government tend to wallow in that area.

The government would like us to believe they know more than we do about these matters. Hopefully they are right, but it would be more comforting if they had to follow the same laws and regulations that "we the people" have to. I know I'm sounding petty, but we elect them to office and then pay them for their service. Doesn't that make us the boss?

Obviously I'm watching way too much TV to think like this. "The needs of the many far out way the needs of the few", a line from Star Trek which maybe our Congressman should start considering, who said you can't learn things from TV? Dreamer that I am it would be nice to think our government was actually looking out for us and not their party's aspirations.

Stop me if you heard this one, another week another sports scandal. This time Oklahoma State is involved with the following allegations. Their players having their grades altered to keep eligibility, money from alumni going to players for good performance on the field, and my favorite female hostess's giving incoming recruits a little something extra. Sounds like another week at the office for college athletics.

Please don't be too alarmed as I'm sure our professional athletes will have another scandal in the near future. Speaking of professionals, there have been some strange bad calls recently in both football and baseball, who knows maybe the officiating will come into question. The conspiracy theorists are starting to huddle, get the pun?

Let's move on to our banks. Through the years I have tried several different banks for various reasons. For years no one bank seemed to offer all the features which I like/need them to do. Free checking was always a big plus for me and now most banks have that feature. Happily they all have online banking with multiple options.

One feature I truly enjoy is "direct deposit". My money is in my account on pay day, no waiting lines, no deposit slips, no waiting period for the check to cash. I can transfer money from checking to savings or vice-versa. The majority of my bills have been set up so that I can schedule and pay them online. They even keep the account balanced for you so even if you forget to right a bill down you can see it online. It is almost foolproof now that you can make deposits at the bank with your ATM card, instead of filling out a deposit slip and making a mistake on the account number.

I'm talking automation at its finest as long as you find one with no hidden fees. These fees can be as bad as the airlines if you're not careful. I can happily say that I'm a gold card customer at my bank with no fees and can do most transactions from my home computer. I know, if things are so great why would I be bringing them up in the "Rant" chapter?

With all those positive features my bank still found a way to shoot itself in the foot regarding my solid credit. Praising me for my good business and credit standing with them they sent me a letter telling me I qualified for a Home Equity line of credit and they also told me the amount I prequalified for as well.

For the record both my wife and I have credit scores over 800 points. If you have ever tried to borrow money for anything you know these scores are holy cow great. We also have no debt as in car payments and no mortgage on the house we live in. When we brought the letter the bank had sent us to apply for the preapproved credit line the bank consultant checked our status and thought this would be a slam dunk.

Again let me reiterate that the bank had sent us a letter for this credit line and the amount. We were told someone would drive by the house within a couple days for a quick appraisal and 3 to 5 days from there the line should be approved. Their letter said it was already preapproved, but this was normal procedure.

Cynthia is a Real Estate agent and assured me this was standard procedure to make sure the house was actually there and not falling down. Even though we had only lived in the house a few months we had made some significant improvements as in new roof and kitchen. She felt the house would appraise at about 2-1/2 times the equity line that was being offered to us.

We didn't need the money, but felt it was a nice cushion to have in case of emergency. Again the bank had suggested the line to us with their original letter.

Early the next week the appraiser stopped by, checked the house from the outside and asked me a couple questions. I mentioned we had also put in a new oil burner along with the roof and kitchen upgrades. We let the agent at the bank know he had stopped by and was told it should be a slam dunk from there. Before continuing let me add the house did appraise at that 2-1/2 level.

A couple days later the parade of red tape started. All of a sudden they needed a couple years' tax returns. Then it was showing them how we sold our old house and taken the equity from that sale to pay in full our new house. We needed bank records from get this THEIR bank showing all the transactions. Here's the one that got me the most, the Town tax bill I had scheduled through THEIR online banking system hadn't cleared yet and why hadn't we paid it yet? They were the ones that had sent out the check, but it hadn't been cashed by the town yet. Even though the transaction showed on my account as pending this was a RED flag.

Hello, you sent us the preapproval, now I'm starting to feel like part of a dog and pony show. A few days later the town cashed the check and we let the agent know. The 3 to 5 day slam dunk procedure took over a month. My wife joked she had closed houses faster than we got this equity line.

Hold on I'm not done yet. Have you seen that commercial with the man standing in the bank and the automated teller is reciting what they consider business days to him, you know Monday through Friday? We finally got the approval and signed the papers on Saturday. Since Saturday was not a business day the transaction would go on record Monday. There was a 3 day waiting period before the transaction was finalized and we could have access to the money.

On Thursday I checked online to see if the equity line had been added to my account, but it wasn't there. We had to withdraw a portion of the equity line to secure the deal which was why I was a bit anxious about not seeing it with my other accounts. After the long wait I really didn't want a mistake on my part voiding the line.

Cynthia had a few checks to deposit so off to the bank I went. I didn't want any mistakes so I figured I would find out what was going on face to face. According to the teller the equity line was still pending for its third day.

Here was the explanation. Since we signed on Saturday the first business day was Monday, but that didn't count as one of the 3 business days. I still don't get it, but tomorrow will be over 6 weeks for this nice easy slam dunk transaction to become official. Again this all started with the banks preapproval letter to us.

On occasion you can be required to have a certified bank check to show your proof of funds. This happens a lot in Real Estate. If I understand this transaction, it takes your cash and verifies it as a certified check. Most banks charge you a fee for this check; personally I have paid as much as $10.00. The money is no longer in an account until that certified check is cashed.

Even if you deposit this check in the bank it was certified from it takes 5 to 7 days for it to clear. Some banks offer a percentage of the money sooner, but not all until the 5th or 7th day. So where is that money for those days? Technically it is not in anyone's account until that check clears. Yet you paid money for a special check to verify funds that are now in limbo.

The housing market is crazy these days and there are many bargains for "cash" buyers. However they don't actually take cash, but a certified bank check to show proof of funds. If you are selling your house to a cash buyer the closing attorneys will not do cash transactions, yes I asked.

Now if you take that check and use it to buy another house within that 5 to 7 day window they will recognize the check as cash. However if there is a balance due in your favor the waiting period still exists. That business day thing is also part of the 5 to 7 day ordeal.

Hopefully you followed along the money trail. So here is the big question I would like answered. How much money are the banks making off that week when the money is in limbo? Remember that's every time a house is sold. Nice racket they have going wouldn't you say?

16

SAYING'S OR WORDS OF WISDOM

Through the years I have come across a few, whether from books, speeches, movies, songs or just listening to people talk. Again my quotes may not be word for word accurate, but I think you will get the points that are trying to be made. Almost everyone has their little "words of wisdom" they have picked up through the years. Some are more famous than others, and then some of their own thoughts thrown in or embellishing the point.

Personally I have a few words that you will not find in the dictionary, but my family knows them well. Some advice for anyone using a word they invented to describe something, you might want your children to know it's not real word. A good example comes from the Three Stooges, "ana-cana-puna". For those familiar with the Stooges you know this could mean almost anything as an added ingredient to a mixture. I have no idea if my spelling is close, but watch an episode and you will probably hear the word used at some point.

I very rarely cook, but I have been known to mix a cocktail or two. If you ask me what's in it ana-cana-puna will be one of the ingredients. This is probably a good time to mention I dance to a different drummer. I am set in my ways and I don't have a problem calling them as I see them. Cynthia is a good buffer for me when we are around people who don't know me or just casual friends.

If someone looks a little befuddled by something I've said or done she will try to explain. As she puts it, "after all these years I speak fluent George". You can substitute Porky, Grumpy or several other adjectives for George depending on the company or situation. Both daughters understand most of my sayings and quirks, thus they just shake their head or utter "dadddd".

Our oldest daughter Jacquelyn grew up during the "Mash" reruns. In the 80's there would be two or more on different channels every night. They had some great lines and Cynthia and I would plagiarize them quite frequently. It got to a point that if Jacquelyn didn't understand something we said and we were laughing about it then she would ask "is it a Mash thing"? For years the answer would be yes.

One of my favorite scenes involved Hawkeye confined to house arrest and his dimwit roommate Frank trying to harass him about it. He stood in the doorway and started jumping in and out of it saying "I can come in, I can go out, in then out." Whenever one of the girls were grounded or had to stay in their room I would go to the doorway and mimic that scene. Yes I was a bit crude.

Did I mention both daughters feel they should have therapy because of me? I always tell them I just liked to spread a little joy when the opportunity arouse. They still aren't amused with that one.

So let's move on to a word I use for duck sauce (sweet-n-sour) at a Chinese restaurant, "huna-huna" sauce. When at the restaurant I would ask Cynthia to pass it to me with a simple request, "pass the huna-huna". When getting take out, I would remind her to ask for extra "huna-huna" sauce with our order. Thus Jacquelyn never actually heard the correct name for it.

I'm sure you can see where this is going as in she was out with friends when she was older and they brought her to a Chinese restaurant. Yes she asked one of them to pass the "huna-huna" sauce and they looked at her in an odd way, or as I would put it "like she was a wackadoodle".

They had a nice laugh at her expense and when she got home she read me her version of the riot act. When she was done with her lecture I asked her if they ever passed her the "huna-huna" sauce and started laughing. She was not amused then and her friends still joke with her about it. When they do I get the thanks "daddd" phone call. I'm still not paying for therapy.

Growing up my family was dys<u>fun</u>ctional, so I'm just passing it on with a little more stress on the "fun". I told you earlier my family considers me "a piece of work". I like to consider it a "work in progress". Please keep the headshaking to a minimal as the fun is just getting started.

"Are you kidding me", seems to come out of my mouth a lot the last few years. When I start a conversation with this phrase you can expect it to be about some outrageously dumb act or statement that someone has done. That someone could be a relative as in daughter who did something I consider to be boneheaded (another common word in my vocabulary) or they might be somewhat famous or associated with sports. Let's face it athletes can really peg the act of doing something stupid meter.

It may also involve something I may have predicted and it actually came true or some act of people using bad judgment. It is usually a negative statement and I will follow it up with my rant on the subject. Cynthia will call this statement an "oh boy" as she knows I'm about to go "off" on something or someone. Politicians and/or their politics are an easy trigger for this type of opening statement.

Here is a great example and one that has happened lately. A politician is exposed for sending inappropriate pictures of himself on his phone. Apologizes while acknowledging his poor judgment, then later gets caught "sexting" on his phone, which is also a big no-no in politics. Are you kidding me, this guy still feels he's capable of holding a public office in government. Maybe sanitation or sewage would be more his calling as his mind appears to be in the gutter.

I'm sure you can see how easily this statement can be used with professional or popular athletes as hardly a day goes by that there isn't some "oops" story about one of them. It's the repeat offenders that bring out my best rants. Let's not forget those who berate others for doing a wrongful act only to get caught doing it themselves at a later date or exposed from an earlier date (hypocrite). Driving/ operating under the influence seems to be a common offense. Failing drug tests is coming on as a steady second.

With all these groups I'm sure there are some very smart and admirable people, but sadly the rotten egg gets most of the press. As my dad would say, "more people like to see a train wreck than a train crossing", sad but true.

Having some popular sayings, statements or fashion style (my knee socks) has a way of staying with you as you journey through life. Even as young children our daughters would be a bit full of themselves. At times I would take it upon myself to bring them back to Earth so to speak. I would ask them "do you know what I like about you"? They would think about what they were just talking about or doing and assume it had something to do with that and answer accordingly. To their dismay my answer back was very simple "nothing".

It didn't take long before they too would answer "nothing". I was not shy about when or where I would ask them the question. Needless to say some relatives (especially Cynthia's mother) and friends would gasp in shock and tell me what a horrible thing that was to say to my daughter. My daughters would laugh and say I tell them I didn't mean it with an added "right dad"? At which time I would laugh and sarcastically say "yea right".

Since it worked so well with them I thought I would give it a try with Lily Harmony (the granddaughter also known as bossy Betty). She being 4 at the time didn't quite get the joke of it, go figure. After thinking about it for a few seconds she replied "Grumpy there must be something you like about me"? Cynthia and C.J. (her mother) would tell her I was kidding but when she looked at me I would be shaking my head no. Which would lead to a simultaneous "Grumpy behave" by all three of them.

Now that Lily is 6 she will quickly respond "nothing", then walk over and tell me she knows I'm kidding because her mother told her so and then call me a big kidder. Ok so I'm kidding, I do like that at the end of the day she goes home with her mother, but if I mention it I get a chorus of "Grumpy be nice".

Sadly I get more lectures from Lily than anyone else I know. She crosses her arms and taps her feet while chewing my butt off about something I said to her or did. As Rodney Dangerfield would say *"I get no respect"*.

Add "seriously Grumpy" to those sayings I hear a lot and it's followed by a variety of not so friendly stares. I can take the stares; it's the lectures that wear me down.

Through the years we all have our favorite ways of saying goodbye when family or friends leave. I stole mine from the movie "Princess Bride" and it was said by Billy Crystal. I can't say it's a movie I would recommend watching, but I did come away with this saying, "have fun storming the castle". Both daughters laugh as they are leaving since they saw the movie, other people give me that weird look. You know, the "what kind of whack-a-doodle is this guy"?

Truth be told I have a small group of people I call friends. They know I have an odd sense of humor and have no problem letting it out no matter where I am or the circumstances. Cynthia will tell you that's why I have a small group of friends. I'm a piece of work that I consider to be one in progress. That's my story and I'm sticking to it.

Since I told you my goodbye greeting I should also share my hello greeting, also coming from a movie. This time it's Woody Harrelson in Cowboy Way when he shows up at an exclusive party where no one knows him. Unlike Woody I will use the greeting with men and women, "How's your hammer hangin?" and I save this for friends only. Yes it's crude but I almost always get a smile from the person I say it too. All others get the standard "hi, how are you?" and no I really don't care.

Now aren't you glad that I'm not your relative or you're not one of my daughters? Yes people will point out that fact; some will go as far as to say "I don't know you" and walk away. Usually that's Cynthia or Jacquelyn, as C.J. will just shake her head and walk away. Did I mention I have a small group of friends and don't make many new ones either?

On the bright side I don't get invited to many gatherings of people I hardly know. When I do the guests will either be laughing with me, at me or shaking their heads. If it's the latter, Cynthia will usually escort me out a little earlier than she had wanted. Yes, then its lecture time for me again on the ride home. On my behalf I do try to behave myself and keep my colorful comments to myself when attending strange gatherings.

Like Jekyll and Hyde however, sometimes Hyde comes out. Jacquelyn and I refer to that as the inner "dark side". Seriously I do think I control this other side of me, which sadly I think is my better side. I'm sure everyone has that breaking point or B.S. meter that goes off and they just can't help letting out their rant or opinion. My point is just a little lower than most. Another good point about being with Cynthia for over 35 years is her grasp of when I'm getting to that point. She's been known to swoop in and save me from a conversation that was about to get let us say interesting.

A popular texting term is OMG! I do not text, nor do I know how to text, nor do I care to know how to text. If you haven't guessed I'm one of those rare people who do not talk on the phone unless by necessity. Cynthia and the girls call that necessity an all the time thing for them. I call that a female trait. For the record my cell phone is a flip-top that doesn't take pictures and I don't even know the number, I use it when traveling.

So back to OMG, which I have changed to OH MY G! My wife and daughters have found my version of the text to be hilarious, because I say it out loud and don't have a clue about texting lingo. I don't understand why they find it so funny when I say it, but if you do too, then enjoy a laugh on me.

As I've mentioned before my daughters like to call me a caveman and joke my first pet was some sort of dinosaur. Even the granddaughter is getting in on the act. It's tough to argue with a young child, but I will continue to do my best.

Needless to say my beloved family loves the way I can butcher a popular phrase. When going to a wedding or family gathering they are all quick to remind me not to say or do something that will embarrass them. While most wives ask their husbands to just be themselves when they go out, mine begs me not too.

I like to point out it's hard to make new friends if I can't talk to people. Then they point out that it's my odd and colorful sayings that tend to drive those people away. How many men out there here the plea "dad, don't say anything that will lose us friends"?

When coming from the wife substitute whatever loving phrase she is referring to you as in place of dad. You know depending on her mood it could be your first name or maybe even "honey", which I hardly ever hear. If she's not thrilled with my recent behavior or attitude the name can become quite colorful.

Since I swim in the river of denial, I take anything she calls me as a compliment. Yes that can "piss her off" too. I always tell her she can call me anything, but I prefer it's not late to dinner. No I will not share any of the colorful names she calls me as I'm trying to keep the book P.G.

Here's a popular saying "take time to stop and smell the roses and or coffee" depending on the situation. My take on this would be stop and enjoy life from time to time. I would like to think most people have enjoyable moments in their lives. The key is did they recognize them and enjoy them as they happened or are they just enjoying the memories?

Myself, I would like to think that I did stop and enjoy those moments when I recognized them. It is probably why I tend to have a laid back attitude today. This might sound crazy, but sometimes it's the little things that make those moments both enjoyable and memorable.

Athletes and competitive people tend to point to their victories as great memories. Sadly those memories are low lights for the losers in most cases. I consider myself to be a competitive person. No I don't play any sports, but I do play card games and such with friends and family.

Cynthia would always remind me to be a little less competitive when playing with our daughters. That was easy for her to say, but once we started playing a game I was playing to win. No I did not throw any games when the girls were younger. When they beat me at something, they knew it was on the "up and up" so to speak.

"Up and up" always struck me as a weird way of saying honest. That's the way my parents brought me up. You played to win, but there was no cheating, lying or "dirty pool". No excuses, you won fairly or you lost the same way. I taught my daughters that principle and now my granddaughter is getting the same lesson. Maybe I will address my competitive spirit and lack of grace and decorum when I win or lose at a later time.

I will tell you Candy Land was not a fun game for me when playing against the girls. Two daughters and one granddaughter and I can count the amount of my wins I had without using my toes. Yes they kicked my butt and rubbed it in every time. The rubbing in part they got from me and I still hear about it from the Mrs. Yes I'm one of those guys that throw their hands in the air and prance around after a win. Nowadays the prance has become moving in place, but you get the picture.

"What goes around comes around" seems to be a popular saying in all aspects of life. C.J. likes to refer to it as "karma". She also would like to think that with all the lows in life there will be highs to offset them. Being a horseplayer they say the same thing about all those losing photo finishes being offset by winning ones. If that concept is correct I'm in for some nice wins going forward and yes I'm trying to wait patiently for them.

As for the whole go around come around idea, my view is more on how you approach life. As you get older you find the rode of life to be very bumpy. I haven't met many people who do not have a few things they would like to change or have done different if they had the proverbial "second chance". Life gives you very few do overs or chance to click the "undo" button.

Take this book as an example of someone's life, be it mine. Most of you would do things differently or may have done things differently with some of the same circumstances. On the bright side by reading this book you will find out what may have happened if you did it my way. I still contend to be a very logical person, although I don't always do the logical thing.

Cynthia once gave me a birthday card that everyone who read it laughed their butt off at and said they hoped it was true. It went something like this, "they broke the mold after making you, and then beat the hell out of the mold maker". It might be the best card I ever got.

I can't stress enough how often my wife and daughters give those strange looks and shake their heads at me. Life is not always a "bowl of cherries" and I've gotten enough pits to know for me adding humor when sugar isn't available helps. The old spoon full of sugar helps the medicine go down only I substitute humor for sugar; after all I am a diabetic.

I hope I'm not the only one catching all those sayings/phrases I've been stringing together. If I am then it's surprising you are still reading this book. For those who are still hanging in there so to speak, hope you are getting a few laughs.

The sayings are starting to get a bit corny or cliché' so let me leave the chapter with one I share with my granddaughter. I say "when the going gets tough" then she finishes "the tough get going". Thank you John Wayne and with that I'm going to the next chapter.

17

EDUCATION MORE IMPORTANT THAN YOU THINK

Recently on the news they reported a study in Massachusetts that showed where the students of the state ranked for their grade level. English was at 91% even though it is some students' second language. Sadly the 9% are getting most of the fast food/customer service jobs. Just joking, but it does seem that way from time to time.

Mathematics was at 80%. My question, were they using a calculator during the test? You know where I'm going with this, are the 20% running cash registers or figuring out your change back at the convenient store? How many of that 20% are also the 9%?

Last was Science at 71%. This one did not surprise me. I'm not sure adults would do much better on this one. After all they debate evolution, climate change, energy sources and pollution. Depending on your view on any of those subjects you will find scientists that see either side of the question.

Again the first two subjects are simple to evaluate. You can speak and understand English or not so much, 2+2 equals 4. I know it's not that simple, but my logic is not that far off if at all. Just for kicks how about giving those tests to our Congress people and Senators, their Science grade might surprise us. As for Math let them show me their skills with a balanced budget that works.

Depending on their political party there could be some alarming differences in scores. Being smart or well educated is not a job requirement for public office. Once again knowing the correct answer may not be the party's position on the subject especially when it comes to Science. Again the well-educated might know the correct answer, but is it their view as well?

Education seems to be a big can of worms in this country. Most people agree our children should get a good education, just at what cost. A computer with internet capabilities is quickly replacing newspapers. Both magazines and books can be viewed online as well. Students can just "google" anything and find many options to view regarding the subject.

Communities are cutting the funding of Library's' and not updating them to keep up with the times. Sadly there are schools that have computer rooms instead of a Library. I know I'm a caveman, but do we really want Library's' to go the way of the "DODO"?

The Library was a big part of my education growing up. It wasn't just a place with books for research or reading. It was a quiet place you could go for studying or writing a paper. Librarians could actually help you with any research problems. Some I considered teachers outside the classroom.

We are slowly losing both of these resources. Has our education system taken a giant step forward putting so much emphasis on computer use and skipping over or avoiding some of the basics? I'm serious look how quickly computers are starting to replace jobs.

More and more stores are offering "self-service" checkout. Hello, those registers are computers that are taking someone's job. The more they improve them, the more people will use them until they become your only option. No cash transactions everything will be computerized. The store clerk and bagger will be like Librarian's and go the way of the "DODO".

Progress will become the rallying cry as these jobs disappear. Once it happens in stores, how far away will the fast food industry be with this self-service concept? What happens to that 29% (9+20) from the education ratings I showed above?

If you're not in that 29% there are some positives. The biggest I see is the "no cash needed" to do your shopping. If stores or people don't carry cash that would cut back on robberies, after all it's tough to hold up a computer. How long until everything is done online? Place your order and pay online than go to store to pick it up.

I must admit I do the majority of my Christmas shopping online with help from catalogues. I never leave the house and my purchases are delivered to my door.

Instead of the three R's (Reading, Writing and Arithmetic) Computer Science and its operation could replace the last two. By the way I don't agree with the three R's as only one begins with R. Not to be picky but let's be accurate when talking education (must be the anal in me).

Sorry to ramble so much on the computer thing, but it is becoming a huge factor in our children's education process. Computers aren't cheap and they are becoming a necessity in our education system. Are Computer Rooms going to replace Library's? Hey is this the next big thing? I'm writing this book on a computer.

I missed out on the VHS/DVD store as my wife felt VHS was a fad and would blow over. The money I could have made with that idea still makes me shake my head. I wasn't smart enough for the DOT.com boom. This Computer Room might just be the answer. I will give it some thought once I finish the book.

Can you appreciate how I logically walked through all those steps and came up with that Computer Room idea? For better or worse my old school education helped me through that process not a computer. Whether it's a good idea or not, it's my education that got me to even think about it. Thinking is what education is supposed to cultivate.

Teachers and Professors are the core of the education system. Teachers are the people that are molding our children's education and thought process. From the age of 5 to 18 they spend more time with our children than we do. Most parents admire and appreciate the job they do educating our children.

The pay scale isn't great, the hours can be long and they are dealing with a variety of different behaviors. Patience is a definite job requirement. I'm not going to argue about whether they deserve more pay, but what happens when people stop going into teaching? Who teaches our children? Computers!

Go have a parent/teacher meeting with a computer and see how well that goes. Talk about no gray areas, not to mention people skills Again, they are molding our children's thought processes and helping them prepare for the adult world. Do you want that responsibility? Do you have the time, patience and oh yea education to do it?

Teachers at all levels feel unappreciated and under paid and in many cases they are right. Here's one for you to think about. A college Professor teaching Economics is grooming our future leaders of the finance world. You know, where most of the world's money resides and revolves. At most colleges he will make a lot less than the Athletic Director. Chances are the whole Economics' Department together will make less than said Director. Let's not forget to mention the big name college coaches who in some cases make more money than all the Professors together at that college.

So here's the point, why does it seem Education always becomes the focal point when budget cuts are made throughout government. It's not that people think it's unimportant; they just want a bargain for their buck. Personally I don't think this is where we should be looking for bargains. Remember the old saying "you get what you pay for".

You pay for a cheap education and that is what you will get. Throw in the federal and state education requirements and soon we will have a population of professional test passers'. That's right some teachers will take the easy way and just teach what the requirements call for to pass the test. No thinkers, just tell them what they should say or do and they will spit it back out at you.

You reap what you sow, another sad saying. Hopefully I will not be around to see our next generation or the one after that complaining the computer failed there child.

Stand up and take a stand, does education matter or should we let our children be "yes" people. This is the answer I was taught, yes it matters, no exceptions, anything else is radical behavior. We don't need thinkers just people thinking the same way. I hope I'm way off base on this one. Otherwise computers will soon be telling you what to do.

By the way another shooting today, but it only killed 6 people. In the suburbs of Boston a moron (my term) blew his hands off playing with fireworks. No terrorist threat but they had to investigate as though it was. Sometimes I feel we are chasing our tails like dogs and not seeing the end.

Not sure this is the right way to go with this subject, but what has happened to the medical profession. Somewhere along the line it went from humanitarian to show me the Benjamin's. An aspirin cost $8.00 and you usually are prescribed two when in the hospital. Are you kidding me? Talk about inflation, if you are kept in a hospital for a week you could have bought a nice car for what they charge you.

Yes they expect an insurance company to pick up that tab, but is that really the point. Our country supposedly offers the best medical Colleges and Universities in the world and they charge big bucks for that education. The young men and women who chose this vocation were deemed humanitarians. When did the Benjamin take over the conversation?

I know this is a getting away from the education aspect, but let me share a quick and true story. A friend was in a horrific car accident where a young woman died and he was taken to the hospital unconscious. The Dr. saved his life on the operating table. The next day he found out my friend had no health insurance and confronted him in Intensive Care.

His concern, how was my friend going to pay him, after all he had saved his life on the operating table? My friend answered "if you were in it for the money then you should have let me die, because someone else did and they didn't have a choice either". I know this was an isolated situation, but don't Dr.'s take some kind of hypocritical oath?

Look at how many foreign Dr.'s there are in our health care system. Did they come here for the medical education or the money that goes with it? I'm sure the answer is somewhere in between, but money is probably still a big part of the answer.

So education leads to better jobs and making a better living financially for those who pursue it, so why are grade school through high school teachers at the low end of the totem pole? Just a little food for thought the next time budget cuts are affecting your school system.

In many communities' a first year teacher makes less than entry level sanitation worker in the same community. One has a college degree the other may not even have a high school diploma.

Here's a nice saying for you to think about, "you get what you pay for". It doesn't just apply to cars, appliances and good booze. If your community is cutting services, teachers and teacher's pay regarding education expect to see the results in your children. Sadly this is where reality really "bites".

As the gap grows between private and public schools regarding education, so will the opportunity for those better paying jobs, look at it from the Employer's point of view. Even if the job requirement is a High School diploma, do you take the public education over the private?

It was over 45 years ago since I entered the ninth grade and it was the first time I noticed children from private schools coming into my public school. Most of them came from religious schools and their parents couldn't afford to pay the tuition for the private high schools and college.

The big thing I remember to this day is how much further ahead they were with all the subject matters. Most of them breezed through that grade with minimal studying to stay on the Honor Roll. It was amazing how better prepared they were for the curricular. They also had much better study habits. I wonder how big that gap is today?

Let me note that our current President graduated from Harvard Law and his predecessor from Yale, neither had an athletic scholarship. Education means something and needs to become more valued than it currently is within our communities.

Yes there are exceptions, just like lottery winners. As Clint Eastwood says in Dirty Harry "are you feeling lucky punk?" Or maybe that education thing needs a closer look. As corny as this will sound one thing I remember more than one teacher saying while going through school is "our children are the future's leaders".

Presently we are told that 1% of our population is the richest in this country. I would be curious as to the percentage that was also well educated.

Speaking from my experience an Associate's degree in Business Management and years of hard work got me to the position of Production Control Manager at a plumbing supply company. I started in the Stockroom and worked my way up.

While working in that Stockroom I would watch several Co Op students work summers in that Stockroom and find office jobs within the company once they graduated. Even the owner's son had spent a summer or two in that Stockroom before I had joined the company. He was a VP when I got there.

It was a proven starting point for advancement in that company. It was a combination of my hard work and an education that taught me how to learn different things that would propel me up the ladder.

Cynthia took the vocational path of seamstress/dressmaking. She added custom drapery making as she progressed with her business. Yes I said her business which she started when I first met her at the age of 19. The Golden Needle is still in business only now it runs from our home instead of a shop.

Together we pushed getting an education to both daughters. We used ourselves as examples of where it can get you in life. Jacquelyn has a BA in Marketing, the other chose motherhood for now. We are proud of both of them and support them as much as we can.

Education, devalue it at our future's expense.

18

SEX, DRUGS AND ROCK-N-ROLL

D on't get excited about "sex" being in the title of another chapter, you'll understand later. My teenage years were the late 60's and early 70's. The music from the 50's was carrying over with its rock-n-roll style, beat and rhythm. The average length of a song was 2 minutes or less. As the music changed so did the name of its dances. The twist was the most popular at the time. The 45 (2 songs on a record) was melting into 33's (albums with multiple songs).

My parents and the generation to follow tended to be cigarette smokers and drinkers. Happily I would stop smoking cigarettes at an early age. They had 45's with 78's (multiple songs but played slower). Back then smoking was allowed almost anywhere. No Smoking signs were few and far between and usually ignored. My father actually helped his father operate an illegal still during his teenage years (prohibition). My generation was bringing Marijuana, LSD and other hard drugs out in the open.

Although they wouldn't consider them "drugs" the drinking and cigarette smoking was there legal vices at the time. They were transitioning from the waltz and jitterbug into rock-n-roll. My parents never did transition to rock-n-roll, Frank Sinatra and Dean Martin were about as wild as they got.

I would joke with them about changing times and music. Now I understand as I don't get Rap, Robotics or whatever it is our kids are listening to now. It's only rock-n-roll, but I like it and still listen to it. I was a late bloomer to the rock-n-roll scene as far as bands went. Please don't laugh but I was a big Elvis fan with a little Rick Nelson on the side. Elvis has survived the ages; Rick died in a plane crash and suffered some legal troubles hindering his promising career.

For the record Rick was a "Teenage Idol" whose family had its own TV show, Ozzie and Harriet. The show was somewhat of a trend setter back in the day. Ask someone my age or older about Tutti-Fruiti ice cream? Rick was the youngest and would sing a song at the end of each show, one of which was Teenage Idol.

Sadly I would hang on to Rick's songs and Elvis's movies and songs while other teens would "Meet The Beatles". For the record Cynthia was and is a huge Beatle fan. Our home has plenty of memorabilia to back up her fandom. We might have all their music on CD's as well.

My taste in music would drift to Rock bands like The Doors, The Rolling Stones, Black Sabbath, Queen and yes even the Beatles. Yes I would discover grass (marijuana) and other drugs along the way. It was a drastic change for the youth of America and I was there for the ride.

Needless to say I was a late bloomer. Although I wasn't real smart or anything like that I'm sure many of my classmates considered me a "nerd". I graduated Weymouth North High School in 1971, the year they split and had a second High School, cleverly named South.

I will go out on a limb and say that there probably isn't one female that I graduated with that remembers me from that school. This would further support my late bloomer phase with sex as well.

Instead of college I would enlist in the Navy right out of high school. I can honestly say those next few years would bring the man out in me. Military life is a big change and one many young men should experience, especially if they have no immediate plans after high school. You meet a variety of people both good and bad and definitely get the meaning of discipline. I entered a boy of 18 and left a man.

During my third year of service my mother was diagnosed with Cancer. I will spare the details, but it was through her body and there was nothing to do but make her comfortable at home. I requested a Hardship discharge to help my father with her care. She would die before I received my discharge. I was able to come home most weekends and she passed on one of the Fridays that I had come home.

That night my father had told me to go out with friends as my mother could no longer recognize anyone. My older sister had flown home to help out and also suggested I go out. When I came home I would learn my mother had passed away and her body was already gone, along with the hospital bed she had been lying in.

My father was waiting for me to let me know she had passed away very peacefully after asking for a drink of water. Over those last two months we watched my mother wither away to the point she weighed less than 60 lbs. Watching someone you love die like this is truly heart wrenching.

It was one of the hardest times in my life. I had broken off my first real relationship with a young woman shortly before my mother got sick and yes it was her choice to breakup. It was not a great time for me.

This may sound strange but it was shortly after her death that I started really listening to rock-n-roll and smoking a lot more pot. There were songs that seemed to fit how I was feeling.

Less than a month after my discharge I would take my first trip with Lucy in the Sky with Diamonds (LSD).

LSD came with many different names: window pane, blotter (which had its own group of names), orange sunshine which was my first and coco puffs which was supposed to be chocolate meth. I wanted to think I was broadening my horizons and took my share of trips. On weekends I would plan them as though I was going away. My body was home but my mind was away.

If my father had known he never told me. A few weeks after my discharge, I would move away from home for a few reasons. My father had brought an old friend who had lost her husband into the house so they would have some companionship. She was doing a much better job at it than me. Honestly it was hard to be in the house my mother had died in just a few months earlier.

My mother's side of the family would basically disown us after learning of my father's companion. As for me I feel that woman probably saved my father from committing suicide. He and my mother had been married for over 30 years.

Looking back at my life this would be one of the biggest turning points and start a series of life altering events for me. I was lost, finding solace in heavy rock like Led Zeppelin, Pink Floyd and all those other bands I mentioned. Only now I found I preferred being stoned when listening to them.

It wasn't long after that I realized I preferred being stoned as my natural state. Some people started their morning with coffee, I preferred smoking a joint. My triangle of life had two sides and I would take the third (sex) whenever a consenting female was willing. Looking back it sounds pathetic, but at the time I was having a hell of a time. I do not recommend this life style, but I was having fun and lived to tell some great stories. I will save them for another book.

Yes I was doing my fair share of drinking along with everything else. Since my mother had been an alcoholic it wasn't something I wanted to think or talk about. Again I found my altered state of mind to be just fine and I was functioning just fine in public when the need arose. Like my depression now, I was swimming in that lovely river of denial. During this time I would have just one steady girlfriend and some occasional hookups (not as many as I would have liked). As it turned out this girlfriend would introduce me to Cynthia and as they say the rest is history.

Cynthia enjoys music and two of her brothers were in a band and I had actually seen them play at bars. How's that for a small world. On a brighter side it was a common interest that I used to develop our relationship. She would not share my enthusiasm with pot or other drugs. Once she fell in love with me as I said in the earlier chapter the sex would follow big time.

Once in love we both made up for lost time in the sex department. Hopefully most of you can remember those "can't keep your hands off each other phase" in a relationship. Not to brag but it wasn't until recent years when that phase slowed up. Damn that bad back and her "hot flashes".

It was during a neighborhood party that Cynthia would kiss and tell a bit and discloses we had made love/sex for 17 days in a row with a few doubleheaders thrown in, forgive my pun. Love is grand.

As many parents will attest having children alters your life style, for me it was a very positive change. Although I will never admit that to our two daughters, I would make some positive changes in my life style. Cynthia probably would have liked to see them sooner and still like to see a few more. Hey I'm still a work in progress.

Since I just jumped through my entire adult life, let me back track a bit. I should probably point out that after leaving the service, I would also stop cutting my hair. Long hair had started to become stylish on men in the late 60's. I started growing mine out the summer of 74. I told you I was a late bloomer.

By the time I was dating Cynthia over 2 years later my hair was well below my shoulders in length. Some would refer to long haired men like me as "hippies".

Personally even though I couldn't sing or play a musical instrument I was "partying like a rock star" and looking the part. In my early courting of Cynthia her mother would recall one of my appearances when picking her daughter up for a date.

As she told it, Cynthia was all dressed up in a nice pants suit and her long red hair nicely cut around her shoulders. I would come knocking at the door wearing dungaree pants with a matching dungaree vest, with NO SHIRT on underneath and my hair was longer than her daughters. What she may or not have known or guessed at the time was that I was also "high as a kite".

When telling the story now I like to point out I didn't follow the trends, but set them. Although I can't say many men were following my vest with no shirt look. However there were a few women that did, only they kept theirs buttoned up tight.

As Easter time rolled around it was time to meet a few members of Cynthia's outer family and Mary (Cynthia's mother) would request I wear a shirt. It was still wintery in New England of course I would wear a shirt. I knew the proper decorum; I had just put it aside for a while. This will sound corny, but Cynthia was bringing me back to the real world I had left when my mother had died.

Anyway off to visit some of her Aunts, Uncles and cousins on her father's side of the family. Small world that it is I would recognize one of her cousins along with a couple of her cousin's friends. I had gone to Junior High with them and they were a grade below me.

It was funny, as the way they gathered in another room and were whispering about me. They recognized what little of my face they could see through my long hair, but couldn't associate George (my name) with the face. Back then my parents had nicknamed me Butch and that was the name they had known me as. You might call Butch an alias that was lost when the family moved from Quincy to a neighboring town Weymouth when I was fifteen.

The thing her cousin Carol would remember was my leading the assembly hall with the "Pledge Allegiance Of The Flag" in my Boy Scout uniform for school assemblies. Talk about going back in time. It brought quite the surprised look to both Cynthia and Mary's faces. There was a lot of head shaking that day and Carol still brings it up from time to time.

As life would turn out she would meet and marry one of my roommates. They have four children and have been married almost as long as Cynthia and I. Both her and Mike (my roommate) would be in our wedding party. She would also make quite the attempt to catch the bouquet, which was caught on film and resides in our wedding album.

How is that for life coming back full circle so to speak? Carol is quick to point out her agreement with Cynthia that I am a "piece of work". Once again I consider that a complement which makes them laugh every time. Am I missing something?

Wow that was quite the ramble, let's get back to rock-n-roll. Before meeting Cynthia I attended a Community college during the day while working full time nights at a warehouse for a super market chain. It was unskilled labor for good money at the time and I was collecting VA benefits for going to school.

This would be one of those truly win-win situations for me. Single, no money problems, health and dental, a job and getting an education. During my first semester I would meet a fellow student Bruce who shared some classes with me. We also shared common interests regarding this chapter's subject matter.

This guy had an uncanny way of acquiring concert tickets for some of the best bands of our time. Thanks to Bruce I actually got to see some of those bands I mentioned earlier and many others. Not only could he get the tickets, but he knew how to get to the places the concerts were at and would do most of the driving.

One of those places was the Orpheum theatre in Boston. It was much smaller than the Boston Garden, where I would see bigger named bands like Aerosmith play. Instead they would have lesser known performers that may not sell out the bigger facilities. One such band was Queen during their earlier years around their 2nd and 3rd album.

I happened to be one of those people who also enjoyed their first album. However "Sheer Heart Attack", the 3rd album would put them on the billboards. I mentioned to be a bit naïve when I was younger and when Bruce scored tickets to see them at the Orpheum I was in. Please don't laugh too hard, but I did not know the lead singer (Freddie Mercury) and other band members were gay.

Let me explain something about my like for rock-n-roll music. I listened to the songs and music I liked, sometimes I couldn't even tell you who the band was, I just liked the song. I was not one of those people who knew all the band members' names for the music they listened too. If I liked a few of the bands songs, then I would gladly go see them perform. I was far from any kind of groupie.

To be honest at the time I enjoyed the drugs I was using at these concerts as much as the bands. Anyway back to that evening at the Orpheum. Bruce had scored 4 tickets, one each for him and his girlfriend, I took one and I honestly can't remember who the fourth person was, at the time I did not have a steady girlfriend.

Although I didn't say anything right away the crowd was dressed a bit on the bazaar side. After closer examination, I would determine that many of those wearing wedding gowns and dresses were men as in most of them. It would be even stranger to be standing at a urinal in the men's room and have guys hiking up dresses and pulling down pantyhose to use a nearby urinal.

I do remember going back to my seat and mentioning something to Bruce about it. He laughed and informed me that we might be the only "straight" men in the audience. As for Queen they rocked the house that night.

I would be lucky enough to see another performer play at the Orpheum on a different night, his name was Dave Mason. He had separated from another band and was on his own so to speak. It was a very mellow concert and he would refer to it as a "jam session".

After an hour or so he would tell the crowd a couple friends had stopped by and he had invited them to come out and jam a bit with him. Again my memory isn't the greatest but I thought he introduced them as Steve Winwood and some guy named Eric Clapton. To be honest at the time I could not recognize either one of them, although I had heard the names. I remember mentioning something about them being pretty good guitar players after hearing them play.

Again it was all about the music for me; if I liked it then I listened to it and bought the albums. Although my main interests were rock-n-roll, I did enjoy some southern rockers and country songs.

Just to tie a few things together in the I'm not kidding stage, let me tell you a quick story regarding the Cape Cod Coliseum. It was the middle of the summer and the temperature was in the mid 90's no exaggeration. Bruce had scored tickets and he was bringing his new girlfriend and I was now dating Cynthia and would bring her.

Dress code was casual to say the least, as in the least as possible without being naked. Trend setter that I was my dungaree vest with no shirt along with long dungaree pants (not sure why I wasn't wearing shorts) would work for me. Not to be undone Bruce's date would also wear a dungaree vest with no shirt or bra on underneath. The difference, I left mine unbuttoned and sadly she had to keep hers completely buttoned.

Once inside she would comment she wished she had worn a tee shirt instead of the vest. Then she elaborated by mentioning most of the other women had followed her no bra idea but were probably much more comfortable than she was. Yes Cynthia would go to the ladies room and remove her bra as well, with a qualifying "it's just too damn hot".

Not that Bruce and I noticed, but it was like being in the middle of a wet tee shirt contest. Oh yes there were 3 bands playing, Outlaws, Heart and no one seems to remember the 3rd. In their defense they played first and most people stayed in the parking lost partying before braving the heat inside the building.

I happily remember several women removing their bras in the parking lot before going into the concert. It was one of those things that once one woman did it a bunch just seemed to follow. Be it the alcohol or drug consumption probably both, most of them were not shy about their clothing change. As I mentioned above Cynthia would wait until we were inside.

Under normal concert conditions Bruce's girlfriend would have been one of the hottest dressed women, that dungaree no shirt underneath thing really worked back then or at least I thought so. As it turned out hers were the only boobs the men didn't get a good view of that day. There's that guy thing again.

Before leaving the concert subject let me offer a public apology to the young lady who would be my blind date for the Aerosmith concert at Boston Garden. She was a friend of one of my roommates' old girlfriends and sadly I can't remember her name. Hi Joanie (roommates ex) if you read this, that was a great concert.

My decision making was not the greatest at the time and I had taken something to enhance the concert experience. It was not my first rodeo so to speak, but not the best first date choices for enhanced entertainment. Aerosmith rocked and she would hold my hand and lead me out when it was over. Aside from being stoned out of my mind I was a perfect gentleman, seriously. There was no second date, go figure.

Back in those days drinking and drugs were not coupled together in the same manner they are today. It wasn't that people weren't using both at the same time, but parents considered them completely different. A parent was concerned if you were caught drunk or drinking, they were worried if they suspected or caught you smoking pot or using any other drugs.

Parents loved me with my short hair and straight laced appearance in high school and in the service. It wouldn't be long after getting out of the service that some of those same parents would cringe if I stopped by to visit their son or daughter. Parents of some of the women I would date once I grew my hair out would have these horrified looks as I escorted their precious daughters' out of the house.

To this day I contest that I acted very gentlemanly with all the women I dated. I only had a few steady girlfriends during those times, but it wasn't because of my lack of manners or respect for women. It was my party like a rock star behavior and attitude.

I would get the same reaction from friend's wives and girlfriends. Yes I was that guy that wives and girlfriends didn't want their men hanging or going out with. Even when I had a girlfriend they preferred double dates rather than letting their man out on the town with me. Comedians like to make the comparisons on tame animals' seeing how their wild counterparts live. Their wives/girlfriends could offer sex thus keeping their men from going out for a couple beers with me.

I admit to being naïve when I was younger and that would include my sexual prowess or lack thereof. Unlike a few lucky young men I did not have that hook up with an older possibly divorced woman to show/direct me in the art of pleasing a woman. Again no laughing, but I knew the basics or at least thought I did. How hard could it be, I had something hanging from my body that would fit into something on the woman's body and I knew what and where both parts resided.

Remember this is the mid 70's and sex wasn't talked about or displayed the way it is today. I will not mention names, times or situations, but I was not aware women could have orgasms in my early relationships. Needless to say once I found out I altered my techniques to help with their "happy endings". Truth be told, I learned a lot from X-rated movies, yes I feel you're snickering. Hey, there wasn't a book, classes or seminars like there are today.

I've been married for over 30 years with two daughters so I must be doing something right. Happily my wife and I educated ourselves the old fashion way, that's right trial and error and of course plenty of practice. The daughters don't like to hear that practice thing.

The moral of the story I still listen to rock-n-roll, my drugs are issued by a Dr. and like most married men I will take sex whenever the wife is in the mood or feeling charitable.

To show I wasn't the only young person naïve in the ways of sex let me share a quick story about a coworker in the late 80's. He was over the house shooting some pool in our family room and Cynthia was in the next room sewing. We were having a couple beers and joking around and I asked him how his girlfriend was doing.

He starts laughing and tells me they just found something out. Yes I thought he was about to tell me she was pregnant, boy was I wrong. True story he tells me that he and the girlfriend had been talking about sex a lot. With a straight face he informed me they both thought that they were having oral sex because they were talking about it.

Cynthia came flying out of the other room laughing hysterically, as was I and asked if he was serious. The answer was yes but please don't tell anyone. Don't worry your secret is safe with me. People to this day find that story funny when I tell it at parties. I know I didn't keep the story a secret, but in my defense would you?

19

OBSERVATIONS, OPINIONS AS I SEE THEM

This will be the last chapter. As I write this chapter I will review the entire book, fixing mistakes and possibly adding a few updates. Earlier today I confirmed with my publisher they will be getting my finished edition the end of next week. It has been fun and I'm hoping added some joy to my reader's lives.

No matter how complicated or crazy your life becomes remember you are not alone. Seriously we all have someone, family, friends or even councilors' to help us through the tough times and share the good times. People have been known to surprise you, just give them a chance, honest they will.

Earlier I wrote about the huge changes that involved my Health care status and provider. I had to change my entire group of Doctors that I had developed over the last 30 plus years. I was not allowed to keep any of them with my Health care changes.

What started as a shaky start with my new health care provider and changing Primary Care physician has developed into a solid relationship that I have now developed a trust in. They have a team of Doctor's that can help me in many different fields.

It was their Cardiologist that diagnosed and helped get me the right treatment. Her team setup all the testing and Pre Op that was required for my procedure. They also handled all the follow up care. Everyone involved treated me like a person not just a patient.

Recently I had to visit their Podiatrist for a toe issue. He actually had to do a procedure right there in his office. The man could not have been more comforting or reassuring as we talked through the whole procedure.

A week earlier I had to visit their Urgent Care office. Talk about efficient and thorough, within minutes they had my information and were starting to run tests and take blood. It was like the Emergency Room without the wait and BS that goes along with it.

A skeptic in the beginning and now I would recommend them to relatives and friends. Look back at the Political chapter and the last entry is about the Obama Health care and the government shutdown. Let me parlay my positive health care change and the shutdown into some thoughts about the government.

Being from Massachusetts I remember a Republican governor by the name of Mitt Romney jamming a health care plan down our throats. His diehard followers and fellow Republicans kept telling us how good it would be for the State and to give it a chance. Some suggested it might be a good plan for the country and in the future we would be a stepping stone State to lead the way, just give it a chance.

As I pointed out in the earlier chapter Romney's health care plan for us was too close to Obama's so now it was not the way to go. Now that the opposing party had a similar view those same people in Massachusetts that told us how good it was now nit-picked the new possibly improved version. They made it a line in the sand point during the election and they lost. Even though the people voted for it they are still fighting it.

I'm not kidding Republicans in our state supported Romney's plan in Massachusetts and if he had stuck with it he might have been elected President. Those same people who talked so highly about Romney's plan were now trying to tell us how it wasn't for the country.

Look at how the economy turned around under the change from Bush to Obama, yes Republican to Democrat. We the people were sinking economically.

The parties agreed something had to be done but the Republicans couldn't agree with any Democratic ideas. They fought, but slowly Obama made some changes and the economy started to go in a forward direction. Let's give credit to those Republicans even though they fought those changes that were now having positive results changed their view and the new view was it was happening too slow and what took so long to implement the changes.

It wasn't that they had better ideas or any at all, they just couldn't give the other party credit. Hey thanks for saving the country but you were kind of slow and so is your process. This is the attitude and behavior that makes people think they would be better off without government.

You know those people who take exception to the government trying to make any changes or suggestions to the status quo. I remember the "keep the government out of my Medicare" slogans, but I think the government made Medicare. How about this one "the government needs to keep their hands off our guns", you know the ones granted us in the Constitution created and supported by the government.

Here's a reality check for all you antigovernment people out there, you lose everything without government. I'll start simple with no food or drug regulations. No expiration dates or safety studies to see if anything is safe. Companies will no longer have to worry about rotating stock. So what if something kills you, did it do what the label suggested? If it doesn't what and who are you going to complain too, the manufacturer?

Look at where we were with labor, employees were literally at the mercy of their employer and their managers. Remember those fair working conditions, wages, and benefits and let's not forget the sexual harassment that went on behind office doors. How many women performed sexual favors for their bosses to keep their jobs or get a raise? Truth be told the latter may have happened to our Grandmothers' more times than you care to think about and they will never tell.

That doesn't even touch our roads, schools, travel in general and my favorite quality of life. There are plenty of countries with minimal government regulations to protect the people. Feel free to relocate if you think you are getting a raw deal.

So what's the alternative keep what you like and trash the rest. Who makes those decisions? Check out the shutdown, all they want is to stop Obama care (it's actually the Affordable Health Care Act), but everything else can pass. Do we really need affordable health care? They don't have a better plan and they don't care people voted for it.

Fox news referred to the shutdown as a slim down. It is costing taxpayers' millions by the day and people are losing services along with some regulatory shutdowns. I don't get the analogy here. When you slim down you are losing something you don't want to get back. Did I mention Fox news tends to get linked to the Republican Party, not sure they are on board with this comparison? Don't worry Fox you have a former member of the View coming to bail you out. Sorry she's a diehard Republican too. Does the term "blind leading the blind" fit here, no offense to the actual blind here?

If I haven't made my point or you are not getting it I'm afraid it will not happen. I like to refer to my country as my house, it has many doors and they all lead out if you are unhappy with what goes on here leave. At least that's what I tell people at my house.

Comedians love to make fun of the government and Bill Maher has made a living at it. He now has a one hour show on HBO to talk about weekly events regarding the news and politics. He finishes the show each week with a rant called "New Rules". He has a variety of guests and they talk over those events. If you haven't watched him, check it out, you might get a few laughs along with an education about some of those events.

I find it amazing how his well-educated guests can have such different points of view on a subject. Some of these guests are College Professors, Political leaders and analysis', Financial Guru's, Actors, Actresses and vary from all political parties including the "Tea Baggers". Check the show out, it may give you an insight as to why the political parties have such different ideas regarding issues of importance.

Stop me if you heard this one, but our government is in a shutdown (slim down according to Fox) not because they don't agree on a budget to support government spending. It's because one party is still trying to stop a Health Care Act that just went into effect. They are using it as leverage to basically hold the country hostage. They all just point fingers at the each other calling it their fault. I feel like I'm back at the school yard arguing with kids.

On a brighter note the hockey season started as did the baseball playoffs. As a sport in general hockey people must have the biggest inferiority complex. I know a crazy change in topic, but I find it a bit sad how little press hockey gets from the sports media, not that I watch or follow it either. Just thought I would give it a quick plug.

Recently I had a follow-up appointment with my back specialist to make sure my medication changes were having a positive result. During the exam I pointed out a bruise on my forehead that I couldn't remember getting, but it hurt worse than the back at the time. I was asked if I felt "safe" at home?

I'm over 60 years old and have had a variety of injuries including concussions and this was the first time anyone in the medical profession had asked me that question. Apparently this is a touchy area of which they take very seriously and I knew it called for a serious answer on my part. When I told Cynthia about them asking the question she gave me a serious look and asked if I gave them a serious answer.

I assured her that I let them know everything was fine at home to which she responded, good, otherwise she would have had to beat the "you know what out of me". After which we both started laughing and now it's become a big joke between the two of us. We both know how serious the issue is, but it doesn't apply to us and we are able to make fun of it. I told you we are a bit dys<u>fun</u>ctional when it comes to these types of situations.

Life is a one-time journey, have some fun, just not at someone else's expense, unless of course their family or good friends. If you can't joke with them life would be very boring. Beside politics comedians get their best material from their own families and experiences.

My parents liked to point out how so many things change and how quickly those changes happen. They were referring to cars and televisions and how electronic devices were starting to help in the work place. Going from black and white TV to color was huge back in the day. The car phone and idea of a portable version were just something you saw on Sci-Fi shows.

I wonder what they would think about cell phones and computers that we have these days. Talk about things changing. Both have new and improve versions yearly sometimes sooner. The daughters' think I'm a dinosaur because I still have a flip top phone and can't text. I'm happy with my Window's 7 as well.

Heck by the time I understand how to do the basics on these devices they change them. New and improved my butt, they might be faster and do more with the "apps", but I still like the KISS method. There is nothing simple about these improvements.

The younger generations will need to adapt to these technology changes as they happen or join me at the back of the pack. Don't get me wrong I understand most of these changes are for improvement. I'm just frustrated that by the time I'm getting good using something there are several newer versions.

On the bright side I save money on video games. I don't know how to play them and don't care to learn, so I don't buy them. My granddaughter is quick to point out how well she is at playing some of those games and has even offered to teach me. Fat chance I'm going to let her show me how to play a game so she can beat me at it.

What has happened to playing cards like rummy or cribbage, solitaire on the computer? I played chess in high school, but now it's just a game offered on the computer. Call me old fashion, but I think our children are losing a great experience playing games on computers and not face to face with friends or competition.

We need to bring that human connection back into our children's lives. Some of these video games are extremely violent and can be very inhumane. Is it possible that the lack of human contact is making our children more violent in the real world? They see it in games, but are they missing the connection between games and real life?

Both of my daughters' no longer watch the news or read newspapers. They get weather updates on their phones and check movie and TV updates there as well. They are quick to point out how violent and destructive the news tends to be and if they wanted to see violence they would play a video game.

Again call me old fashion, but we are losing the upcoming generation when it comes to the Media. Newspapers and magazines can be viewed on line. Current events are a click away on any computer or phone, if they care to watch them, which they don't. I truly believe upcoming generations are going to lose out on the way people bring us our current news events.

Are we going to the self-checkout aisle to avoid human contact? Automation has its place, but how many jobs will it cost along the way? I'm all for progress but let's not leave the human behind. A computer can calculate a decision, but people can make humane decisions.

If we are what we eat and do what we see (video games) then big changes are coming our way and not in a good way. Enough with the philosophical babble, time to wrap things up.

This book touched on a variety of subjects that affected my life and hopefully some of yours. I may or may not have handled things the right, smart or conventional way. Life is a work in progress just like me. By the way putting them into words to create this book wasn't as easy as you might think either.

For those who read the book I hope you got some laughs and insights. As the title suggests these views are from a man/guy, not all men. Agree or disagree, this is how it happened and worked out for me.

Lastly to those big-wigs at ESPN, the charity could be breast cancer and you might be surprised how positive a response you get from your female sportscasters and reporters. Yes it's another plug for that calendar depicting their beautiful women.

ABOUT THE AUTHOR

I was born in Boston, May of 1953. I grew up in the nearby suburbs. First Quincy Point, then at 15 over to Weymouth, where I would graduate High School at Weymouth North class of "71", I don't expect many for my fellow grads to recognize my name or picture if they saw it.

I went into the Navy at 18 and served almost 3 years. I had two jobs since that are worth noting. I picked orders at a warehouse for a grocery chain for close to 7 years. Graduated from Massasoit Community College before moving to my next job, where I would spend 29 years working my way up the ladder from Stockroom clerk to Production Control Manager.

I've been married to my wife since 1979 and we have two beautiful daughters'. Also noteworthy I would grow a beard in August of "79" which I also still have covering my face, it's the caveman in me.

I don't tweet or text, but I do have a Facebook page. Find me at George Robbins II as I will have updates from time to time and will answer questions. I can't promise you will like or agree with the answers.

Lastly, I'm just a man, no fame, no glory, just someone keeping it real. You will also note that English was not my best subject. To that my apologizes to any old English teachers that may recognize my name, which I doubt will happen.

DEDICATION

To my entire family, wife Cynthia, daughters' Jacquelyn and Carolyn J. and of course, the three dogs, Penny Lane, Abbey Road and Eleanor Rigby. I told you Cynthia was a Beatles fan and I expect Lovely Rita to join us soon. It took a while for me to "get it", but family truly is everything.

Prepare to enter the mind of one man and share some of his experiences in *Ramblings, Rants, and Ravings of a Man*. In this collection of essays, author George Robbins touches on a variety of subjects that affect many of our lives—driving, sports, politics, family, and even his fight with depression. The events are depicted as he remembers them, though he has done his best not to embarras friends and family. With straightforward honesty, he shares some of his deepest thoughts and beliefs on a wide rage of topics.

For example, he explores how he and his wife handled their children with humo Although his recollections aren't always fun, he does try to find a humorous side whenever possible—even when it's at his own expense. He refers to himself as "a piece of work" and "a work in progress" throughout the book, explaining his reasoning for this view of himself.

From road rage to raising children, *Ramblings, Rants, and Ravings of a Man* offers one man's honest thoughts—possibly a bit more honest than most. Robbins recalls his sixty years, including the good, the bad, and the unbelievable

George Robbins was born in Boston and raised in the nearby suburbs. He spent three years in the US Navy. After his service, he accepted a position where he moved from stockroom clerk to production control manager. He and his wife have two daughters Robbins' first published book, *"Tips for Playing the Horses,"* is available on Amazon.

iUniverse®
www.iuniverse.com